100'

0% F

~ ·atnolic

MW01002898

Second Edition

The OLD CATHOLIC CHURCH has been around for hundreds of years, but few people today know about it. Larger groups that use the word "Catholic" rarely like to admit its existence, but it does exist. It is completely Catholic, but without the pope, the Inquisition and all the guilt.

Archbishop Wynn Wagner introduces you to the beliefs of this small group of Catholics with their modern philosophy that is wrapped inside a very traditional liturgy. Expect to be amazed at the spiritual tools that are available to you today. When someone says you can't marry because you are gay, or that you can't be a Catholic priest because you are married or a female: read this book and find your answer.

"Some books that introduce a religion are dry and boring. If that is what you want, don't look in these pages. Archbishop Wynn Wagner brings the Old Catholic Church to life. This is a "Pilgrim's Guide," and the archbishop is the first to let you know that he is just another pilgrim. When he doesn't know the answer, he tells you. He tells you in ways that may leave you chuckling. When he talks about the majesty of our Old Catholic Church, he speaks with the authority of someone who walks-the-walk. The "Pilgrim's Guide" is more than a simple introduction, it is a tour of what can be your spiritual life with a tour guide who lives the subject matter on a daily basis."

Archbishop Michael V. Seneco, First Presiding Bishop
North American Old Catholic Church

Also from Abp. Wynn...

TAROT for Christians:
Lessons from Christ's Fool

Recovering Catholic:
How to be Catholic Without Being Roman Catholic

The Complete Liturgy
for Independent, Mystical and Liberal Catholics

The Rites of the Old Catholic Church

Shameless Self-plugs from
Mystic Ways Books...

The Divine and Healing Path
Bp. Elijah (Jim Rankin)

A Catechism of the Liberal Catholic Church

Ordo Missae

The Eucharist
(Sacramentary)

Old Catholic Lectionary

A Pilgrim's Guide to the Old Catholic Church

Archbishop Wynn Wagner

Regionary Bishop of the Southern Province USA (Retired)

and

Coadjutor Emeritus of the North American Old Catholic Church

MysticWays BOOKS

ISBN 978-0-9855981-5-0

Mystic Ways Books – www.MysticWaysBooks.com
Dallas Texas 75219

Scripture quotations are from the New King James Version.

Wagner, Abp. Wynn
Pilgrim's Guide to the Old Catholic Church / Abp. Wynn Wagner

1. Old Catholic Church – Doctrines. I. Title

For Ruth and Mychal

Table of Contents

Preface

The words printed here are concepts. You must go through the experiences.

Saint Augustine of Hippo (354-430)

Before I started writing this book, I discussed it with several friends. One of those discussions went like this:

Me   I'm writing a catechism of the Old Catholic Church.

Him   Didn't you already write a catechism?

Me   Yeah, but that was on the Liberal Catholic Church.

Him   You were a priest there, right?

Me   Uh-huh.

Him   And now, you're a priest in the Old Catholic Church?

Me   An archbishop, actually.

Him   An archbishop?

Me   Un-huh. Weird, isn't it?

Him   And you actually joined a church that would admit you as an archbishop?

Me   They don't know me like you do.

Him   But your readers may know you wrote a book about the "competition."

Me   Yup.

Him   I can't wait to see how you dig your way out of this one.

Me   That makes two of us

Just so you know, the Liberal Catholic Church (my older home) was a split from the Old Catholic Church. I didn't make a huge change: just a short swim upstream.

To make things dicier for you, I am not claiming to be an absolute authority on the Old Catholic Church.

Don't get me wrong, one doesn't become an archbishop in a serious-minded national church like the North American Old Catholic Church without a certain degree of wattage. But....

Remember how John Travolta made his entrance in the movie *Michael*? He was playing the part of the Archangel Michael. The first time we see him, he is walking down the stairs chain-smoking cigarettes. When somebody mentions that he does look or act like the typical archangel, Travolta's character says, "Oh, I'm not that kind of angel."

I try my level best. But whatever you are expecting from somebody with the title of archbishop: I'm not that kind of archbishop. I neither smoke nor drink, but I am more comfortable in cut-offs than in the fancy dress required of my job.

This book covers my own personal journey as much as it covers anything else. It points out some pitfalls along the way... pitfalls that I have never actually encountered by doing something stupid, of course, but I have read about these pitfalls and feel it is my duty to pass them along so you don't have to do stupid spiritual tricks, even if they are amusing to all your spouse and friends.

If everybody's really clear on that point, let's get started. This is one heck of a trip!

Introduction

THE ELEVATOR VERSION

The "elevator version" of anything is a summary that you can get through in just the few seconds you spend in an elevator. Because we have the word "Catholic" in our name, most people want to know how we are different from the Roman Catholic Church. So here is the "elevator version" of that:

	Old Catholic	Roman Catholic
Openly gay priests	✔	✘
Closeted gay priests	✘	✔
Marriage after a divorce	✔	✘
Same-gender weddings	✔	✘
Trained/licensed priests	✔	✔
Criminal check on all clergy	✔	✘
Tons of rules for believers	✘	✔

In the Old Catholic Church sexual and gender orientation are not impediments to any sacrament, including Holy Orders and Matrimony.

Of course the Romans have gay priests. They just have to lie about it.

By church law, each lay member's faith is sovereign (NA-OCC).

BEING DIFFERENT

> *We are not to throw away those things that can benefit our neighbor. Goods are called good because they can be used for good: they are instruments for good, in the hands of those who use them properly.*
>
> Clement of Alexandria (150-215)

Unlike other modern branches of Christianity, the Old Catholic Church isn't a "melting pot" with every ladle from the pot looks like every other ladle. The Old Catholic Church is more like a tossed salad, where every bit is going to be identifiable as a distinct item.

Every country has its own distinct Old Catholic Church. Germany has its Alt-Katholiken in Deutschland. In the Czech Republic, it is the Starokatolická církev v Ceské republice. The United States has the North American Old Catholic Church.

The Dutch church can't impose dogma on anyone outside the Netherlands. Swiss bishops have no standing in the operation of the Austrian church. Each of the national churches has its own teachings, practices and traditions.

What's more, each bishop in each national church has more "freedom" than a bishop in another denomination. An Old Catholic Bishop can authorize a liturgy or patron saint that applies only in the bishop's jurisdiction.

On top of that, each lay member's beliefs are sovereign. There is no church authority that can order any individual to believe or act a certain way.

It sounds like chaos, but it works nicely.

Here is something I hear from time to time: "if this church was able to make room for somebody like me, then I am responsible for making room for somebody like you."

In fact, it is the way the Christian church started. Bishops were responsible for a jurisdiction, but each individual was responsible for himself or herself and for helping the next guy.

The arrangement is weird enough that we have to call it a mystery. A mystery is something we can partly understand, but nobody can grasp the entire meaning completely.

Somehow the church as a whole is the *Mystical Body of Christ*, and each national church stands as an incarnation of that Mystical Body, and every individual personifies (brings to life) the Mystical Body. The Church is Christ-ness, and you are what makes this Christ touchable. If a hungry person reaches out, you are there to be touched. If a prisoner cries for God, your ears are what hear the cry. If a sick person seeks help, you are the one who is there with comfort.

Taken as a whole, this isn't like Christ. It is Christ, and you are as integral a part as anybody. What are you supposed to be doing? I have no idea: I barely know what I'm supposed to be doing, for crying out loud. I do know that God needs you. God needs all of us.

And I know one other thing: what you're supposed to do is something you can do. Nobody is given a load that can't be carried, and nobody is given a load that is useless or helpless. When Mother Theresa of Calcutta was working with the old and the sick, somebody snarled "You can't help these people: you're old and sick yourself." Mother Theresa of Calcutta responded, "I wasn't called to be successful. I was called to be faithful."

And so it goes.

What We Believe

This "What We Believe" section was written by Bishop Elijah (Jim Rankin), the Old Catholic bishop of San Francisco, California. The bishop died in 2005. The text of this chapter is from his book A Divine and Healing Path (Rankin 2009).

It covers the CREED, which comes to us from the Latin word that means "I believe."[1] A denomination's creed is a brief summary of what it teaches. In this case, the creed is the Nicene–Constantinopolitan Creed, first written at the church council in Nicaea[2] in the year 325 and tweaked a bit at a church council in Constantinople[3] in the year 381.

It differs from what some modern denominations call the Nicene Creed. The Roman sect, for example, made some unilateral changes to the creed, and they were changes serious enough to split the Christian church in two. Rome's changes are directly linked to the formation of both the Italian church (called the Roman Catholic Church) and the rest of Christianity (collectively called the Orthodox churches).

The Old Catholic Church dates to a time before this split.

---

1   The latin word is "credo"

2   Nicaea doesn't exist today. It is near the town of İznik, Turkey.

3   Now called Istanbul, Turkey.

In Bishop Elijah's text, you will see words — such as Theotokos — which we think of as an Orthodox word. The bishop is using terms from the point of view of an undivided church. Don't worry, all those Greek-based words will have footnotes.

Now, the late Bishop Elijah to summarize what we believe…

Symbolon

From A Divine and Healing Path, by Bishop Elijah (Jim Rankin)

If **kerygma**[4] tells us we walk a path, the catechesis of the Symbol of Nicaea and Constantinople tells us with whom we walk it. The apostolic faith came to the Church as an internal mystery, Tradition, which was not held fitting for the unbaptized — or even for the learners (catechumens) who were preparing for baptism. "Holy things are for the holy." The Symbol, which the Western Catholic refers to as the "Creed," was deemed worthy to be given out to the learner, while such internal prayers as the "Our Father" and the Eucharistic mysteries were for the initiated Christian only.

The Symbol, which like an icon participates in the reality it expresses, is both kerygma and catechesis. To the initiate, it expresses the depths of the mystery of the Christian path, or way of life. For the catechumen, it is both an introduction to the concept of a path or way of life, and a formal introduction to the central mysteries of the Catholic faith.

The Symbol of Faith, first introduced at the Council of Nicaea (325 AD), and completed in its present form at the Council of

---

4 Kerygma (Greek: κήρυγμα, kérugma) is the Greek word used in the New Testament for preaching (see Luke 4:18-19, Romans 10:14, Matthew 3:1). It is related to the Greek verb κηρύσσω (kērússō), to cry or proclaim as a herald, and means proclamation, announcement, or preaching. The New Testament teaches that as Jesus launched his public ministry he entered the synagogue and read from the scroll of Isaiah the prophet. He identified himself as the one Isaiah predicted in Isa 61 (Luke 4:17-21). The text is a programmatic statement of Jesus' ministry to preach or proclaim (Kerygma), good news to the poor and the blind and the captive. [Wiki]

Constantinople (381 AD), is a capsule presentation of the Catholic faith. Its authority is complete; for all the Catholic Church receives all Catholics, of whatever tradition, recognize it, and the councils that enacted it as ecumenical.

Symbolon refers in Greek to being "thrown together," implying a kernel statement of faith, an icon, which while it expresses the fullness but not the entirety of Tradition, participates in the very faith it expresses. The Western "Creed," referring to the Latin of its initial word, "Credo," focuses on the statement of belief itself. The Symbol is reverenced so highly that it precedes the Eucharist in almost every Liturgy, and it is said that according to one custom, not even the priest celebrating the Eucharist was allowed to receive Communion without first reciting the Symbol.

However important as an expression of the true and Catholic faith, it would be a serious mistake to see in the Symbol a set of propositions to which one must give moral and verbal assent, to be considered an orthodox Catholic. Rather, it tells us with whom we walk, and the eschatological hope in which we walk. And the "whom" and the hope are one.

The Nicene Creed, or Symbol of Faith, is the great statement of the early Church of its journey in this world, and of its understanding of that daily journey as a body walking with that Someone who both accompanies us, and awaits us at journey's end as our salvation and our hope. We have already begun to live in both worlds, says the Church — in this world, and in the world to come. Herein lies the mystery of the Incarnation ("and the Word became flesh"), our firm belief in the redemption of the Cosmos entire, and our own eternal destiny ("the resurrection of the dead, and the life of the world to come"), in which hope, as of an accomplished redemption, we already live.

> *...and calling to mind all that has been accomplished for us: the Cross, the Grave, the Resurrection, the Ascension, the Seating at the Right Hand, and the Second and Glorious Advent, which is to come.*
>
> Anamnesis, from the Liturgy of Saint John Chrysostom

The Way of a Christian is witnessed in the apostolic proclamation of the glad tidings of Jesus Christ (kerygma), carried forth in the Church by the leading of the Holy Spirit (Tradition), and is encapsulated for the learner (catechumen) as well as the Church as a whole in the symbolon enacted at Nicaea (325 AD), and completed at Constantinople (381 AD).

Nicaea and Constantinople address the "Who" and the "why" of the Christian way; or better, tells us with Whom we walk, and with what expectation.

> *...for I know whom I have believed and am persuaded that He is able to keep what I have committed unto Him against that Day.*
>
> 2 Timothy 1:12 (NKJV)

The Symbol of Nicaea–Constantinople

We believe in one God, the Father Almighty, Maker of heaven and earth, and of all things visible and invisible;

And in one Lord Jesus Christ, the Son of God, the Only-begotten, Begotten of the Father before all worlds, Light of Light, Very God of Very God, Begotten, not made; of one essence with the Father, by whom all things were made:

Who for us men and for our salvation came down from heaven, and was incarnate of the Holy Spirit and the Virgin Mary, and was made man;

And was crucified also for us under Pontius Pilate, and suffered and was buried;

And the third day, He rose again, according to the Scriptures;

And ascended into heaven, and sits at the right hand of the Father;

And He shall come again with glory to judge the quick and the dead, Whose kingdom shall have no end.

And We believe in the Holy Spirit, the Lord, and Giver of Life, Who proceeds from the Father, Who with the Father and the Son together is worshiped and glorified, Who spoke by the Prophets;

And We believe in One Holy Catholic and Apostolic Church.

We acknowledge one Baptism for the remission of sins.

We look for the Resurrection of the dead,

And the Life of the world to come.

Amen.

In modern times, the "We" of the ecumenical council of Nicaea has become an "I" — where the Council said: "We believe..." moderns tend to say: "I believe..." Yet, unless the "We" of the Council becomes in fact an "I" — unless each one of us internalizes the faith of the Council, to live it out in its full mystery of unity and diversity, individual and communal, the faith is a lifeless thing. Each of us must take up the mystery, and seek to plumb its depths, treasure it, and guard it.

WE BELIEVE IN ONE GOD

God is One, because the Father is One. Christ, the Logos, is begotten of the Father eternally, before all creation, by some method we do not know, and is begotten in this world as human, as the Scriptures tell. The Holy Spirit proceeds from the Father, by a process we do not know, but which is distinguished from begetting.

Yet, God is One. The Father is the *arche*, or fundamental principle of godhood, and while the Son and the Spirit arise from this origin, they arise eternally, and are co-extensive in time with the Father. In the Father lies the Oneness of God, who otherwise comes to us as Persons, as a Trinity.[5] In God there is unity, and diversity.

Yet, as Tradition says, God is unknowable in essence, and is beyond all our concepts and categories — and will be so, forever. God is the Abyss.

God is personal. That is, God comes to us as person, as persons. Whatever the unfathomable essence of God, we experience God as distinct persons, and are told that these persons are real, not symbolic, not modes or operations, not "masks." (Do I accept Jesus Christ as my "personal" Savior? Of course!) The personhood of the Father rests in the fact of being the origin, beginning, ruling principle and fundamental ground of God, the One.

The God of Christians is not abstract, and the oneness of God is not abstract, or empty. The oneness of God is personal.

THE FATHER ALMIGHTY

God is Father in Jesus Christ, and in us. God the One, who is the foundation of godhood, begets the Christ the Logos, the eternal Word, and in the world of time, creates us, and adopts us as children:

> *For you are all sons of God, through faith in Christ Jesus. For as many of you as were baptized into Christ have put on Christ. There is neither Jew nor Greek, there is neither slave nor free, there is neither male nor female; for you are all one in Christ Jesus. And if you are Christ's, then you are Abraham's seed, and*

---

5 The word "trinity" means three. In Christianity, the Trinity refers to God the Father, God the Son, and God the Holy Spirit.

heirs according to the promise.

Galatians 3:26–29 (NKJV)

Christ, who is consubstantial[6] with the Father as to his god nature, is consubstantial with us as to his humanity; and thus his Incarnation is the beginning of a great mystery, which is revealed in the fatherhood of God, Father to the Word in the divine order and Father to Jesus in the human order; Our Father.

We receive the Spirit that leads us to cry: "Father!"

> *Now I say that the heir, as long as he is a child, does not differ at all from a slave, though he is master of all, but is under guardians and stewards until the time appointed by the father. Even so we, when we were children, were in bondage under the elements of the world. But when the fullness of the time had come, God sent forth His Son, born of a woman, born under the law, to redeem those who were under the law, that we might receive the adoption as sons. And because you are sons, God has sent forth the Spirit of His Son into your hearts, crying out, 'Abba!' ('Father!') Therefore you are no longer a slave but a son, and if a son, then an heir of God, through Christ.*

Galatians 4:1–7(NKJV)

East or West, almost all the great Eucharistic liturgies place the "Our Father" just after the prayers of consecration, and before Holy Communion. This is an essential part of the kerygma, the apostolic tradition of the Church, whereby we affirm the adoption we have as sons and heirs of God in Christ Jesus (divinization).

Our approach is humble, and without arrogance or pride. We do not presume, but neither are we shy with regard to the Father.

---

6   of the same essence

We are God's holy people, of whom it is said: "Holy things to the holy!"(Chrysostom 5th Century) We stand where we have a right to stand: in our Father's house, at our Father's table.

"Formed by the Word of God, and taught by divine precept," says the Roman Catholic Mass, "we make bold to say: 'Our Father…'" We have heard Gospel and Epistle, listened to a sermon or homily, proclaimed the Mystery of Faith during the consecratory prayers of the Canon; and now, as Christ himself gave us the words, we pray the "Our Father" before taking Communion.

"And when you pray, do not use vain repetitions as the heathen do. For they think they shall be heard for their many words. Therefore do not be like them. For your Father knows the things you have need of before you ask Him.

> *In this manner, therefore, pray:*
> *"Our Father in heaven,*
> *Hallowed be Your name.*
> *Your kingdom come.*
> *Your will be done*
> *In earth as it is in heaven.*
> *Give us this day our daily bread.*
> *And forgive us our debts,*
> *As we forgive our debtors.*
> *And do not lead us into temptation,*
> *But deliver us from the evil one.*
>
> Matthew 6:7–13(NKJV)

The Liturgy of St. John Chrysostom is typical of the Eastern liturgies, and makes the same point the Roman Mass does, that we acquire an intimate confidence in God, in His mercies and compassions, having a spirit of adoption that allows us to approach the Throne of Grace: "Unto you we commend our whole life and our hope, O Master who loves mankind; and we beseech you, and pray you, and supplicate you: make us worthy to partake of the heavenly and terrible Mysteries of this sacred and spiritual table, with a pure conscience: unto remission of sins, unto forgiveness of transgressions, unto communion of the Holy Spirit, unto inheritance of the Kingdom of Heaven, unto boldness toward You, and not unto judgment or condemnation.

"And vouchsafe, O Lord, that with boldness and without condemnation we may dare to call upon you, the heavenly God, as Father, and say: 'Our Father...' "

And this affirmation immediately arises out of our spiritual preparation, and immediately before Holy Communion. The "Our Father" is a participation of the people in the divine life, and the proclamation of the apostolic witness as our own. It is kerygma, not catechesis.

The relationship of God the Father and God the Son demonstrates our relationship to God, by adoption: we are called upon to know, love and serve God, as a son would his father. And not only we as individuals, but we as the Israel of the Lord of the Old Covenant, and the Church, the Israel of the New Covenant.

> *You, O Lord, are our Father; our Redeemer from Everlasting is Your name.*
>
> Isaiah 63:16 (NKJV)

> *For I am a Father to Israel, and Ephraim is My firstborn.*
>
> Jeremiah 31:9 (NKJV)

> *Have we not all one Father?*
>
> Malachi 2:10 (NKJV)

> *Do not call anyone on earth your father: for One is your Father, He who is in heaven.*
>
> Matthew 23:9 (NKJV)

Until, at last, God the Father speaks to us through His Son, in whom we have the adoption:

> *For to which of the angels did He ever say: 'You are My Son, today have I begotten You'?*
>
> Psalm 2:7 (NKJV)

And again:

> *"I will be to Him a Father, and He shall be to Me a Son?"*
>
> 2 Samuel 7:14 (NKJV)

MAKER OF HEAVEN AND EARTH

> *In the beginning, God created the heavens and the earth.*
>
> Genesis 1:1 (NKJV)

God the Father created the world in Christ Jesus, through the activity of the Spirit.

Creation was not, as with pagan gods, from existing matter, nor from an over-riding Necessity that ruled the gods. Rather, it was ex nihilo,[7] as the Chrysostom and Basil Liturgies emphasize. God does not operate upon co–eternal Matter, or under the bondage of an external Necessity, but is totally free, then and now, to act. All things exist or do not exist out of the will of God alone. Necessity, to the degree that it exists, is an expression of the internal structure of what God brings into being.

Creation ex nihilo, should not be romanticized or misunderstood. The "nothing" of Christian creation is not the no-thing or unmanifest of Asian religions; but is rather an expression of the freedom of God, vis–a–vis creation in the manifest, material

---

7   out of nothing

world. God is present in the world (immanence), but beyond it as well (transcendence), and in no way can God be reduced to a mere part of the world, not even the summation or total of it (pantheism). God is truly Other, God is the Abyss. God is truly free, subject neither to a co–eternal field of Matter nor to an external Necessity.

Georg Hegel

God created ex nihilo, which means, first of all, that God created the world as a free act of His own will, and not from any necessity whatsoever.

Creation ex nihilo reminds us that God is beyond "Being." And if beyond "Being," then beyond its antithesis, "non–being." Nor does Hegel's[8] "Becoming" answer the matter, for while it posits validly a certain knowledge of process within Creation, Hegelian process (Being/Non–being/Becoming) applied to the Deity as if to an object, tends toward Gnostic reductionism, or pantheism.

"Thou art God ineffable, inconceivable, invisible, incomprehensible, ever-existing and eternally the same," says the Anaphora[9] of the Chrysostom Liturgy, "Thou and Thine only–begotten Son and Thy Holy Spirit." "Thou it was who brought us from non–existence into being…" God is alone "the only truly existing God," revealed in Christ Jesus and revealing the Holy Spirit, through whom we have "the gift of sonship," says the Anaphora of the Liturgy of St. Basil.

---

8   George Wilhelm Friedrich Hegel (1770-1831), a German philosopher who taught Idealism. His God was absolute and concrete, not some abstract idea.

9   The most solemn part of the Eucharist, where bread becomes the Body of Christ and wine becomes the Blood of Christ.

God alone is, but God has no name, for to be named would be to be located in the field of the known, creation:

> *Out of the ground the Lord God formed every beast of the field and every bird of the air, and brought them to Adam to see what he would call them. And whatever Adam called each living creature that was its name. So Adam gave names to all cattle, to the birds of the air, and to every beast of the field.*
>
> Genesis 3:19–20 (NKJV)

God makes all things but is not made: neither as Father, nor as Son, nor as Holy Spirit.

OF ALL THINGS, VISIBLE AND INVISIBLE

Pantocrator:[10] if God is the creator of the whole manifest world, so also is God creator of the unmanifest.

We cannot imagine the worlds of God's creation or the extent of it, whether seen by our eyes, or not seen.

In God all things come to have their being, but freely by the will of God, and not of any necessity.

This is what we mean when we say that God created all things ex nihilo. God was under no necessity or compulsion to create, had no inner need: no lack or defect, which mandated creation. It was an act of God's freedom.

The Gods of Olympus were under necessity. Eternal chaos reigned, and they subdued or disciplined it. The creator god of the Greeks was an artisan working upon the co-eternal matter of the Cosmos. To matter and slow time, the gods were subject, as well as man.

The pagan gods were gods of passions, most often human

---

10 All-Creator; All-Container. A term used for Jesus Christ, especial in the Orthodox churches.

passions of the most ordinary sort — or the exaggerations of them. They were filled with jealousies, and resented the cattle they call "men" resisting or presuming upon their state. The havoc wrought upon Prometheus for having brought fire to man is indicative of the rule of the gods, and their jealousy.

In a deeper sense, the Gods of Olympus are little more than the oligarchic[11] model of human society, rendered as a complete cosmology, for the oligarchs of old were privileged elite classes, for whom the broad mass of humankind were as but cattle to their eyes, or tools for their use and desires. Parnassus and Olympus had but little other meaning, in an age when human beings only slowly emerged from the darkness of the primitive human soul. They are the interpretive masks of another society, one whose persistence into the Twentieth Century has virtually turned it into a century of horrors.

God permeates all of Creation; is immanent in it, even while God utterly transcends all Creation, even as God transcends all our ideas, images and categories. God, the Knowable, comes to us as grace. God, the Abyss, the Unknowable, rises above all our ideas and all created things.

God is love, and is not jealous.

God comes to us in Creation, which in turn bears witness in its very contingency to the Eternal Purpose that creates and sustains it.

One cannot "reduce" God to nature, or creation — not even the whole of it. In this transcendence, or this transcendent immanence, which we call "mystery," we understand that God is not a metaphor for the universe as a whole, which we encounter in Benedict de Spinoza (1632-1677) as tendency, and in some religions of the East as a clear proposition.

God is not a metaphor for us.

God is.

---

11 An oligarchy, in a nutshell, is the rule of a few old guys. The word oligarchy (from Greek ὀλιγαρχία (oligarkhía); from ὀλίγος (olígos), meaning "a few", and ἄρχω (archo), meaning "to rule or to command").

In a deeper sense, God is beyond all "is-ing" — beyond all being and existence, altogether. The love of God, which comes to us as Predestination — an eternal purpose of creative good, and good in creation — is an activity of the most holy and undivided Trinity, as a whole.

For, the Father, who is the Uncreated Creator, does not "create" the Son, nor much less, the Holy Spirit. Rather, they are eternally — from "before" Time (outside Time, as created) — "begotten" of the Father, and "proceed" from the Father as from the One Principle, sharing the nature of God, each experiencing a personal being only as God, and each participating in creation.

The Trinity is outside Creation, and creates — as one God, as three Persons. They are eternally God, and even the idea of the Trinity is not adequate to represent them, nor to express the fullness of their love for humankind.[12]

The Trinity is not a process or the result of a process, but "a primordial given." (Lossky 1989, p. 48) The begetting of the Son, and the procession of the Holy Spirit are a "work of nature," according to Athanasius, which John Damascene explains as being opposed to a "work of the will." God comes to us as Person and Persons, as work of the very nature of God, but our creation, and the creation of all things (visible and invisible), is a work of the will of God.

But, here we can pose no necessity in God. The Trinitarian life is an expression of God's internal nature, but is in no wise an act of the will, as is creation — and thus an expression of no necessity.

The revelation or manifestation of God in various attributes, such as love or creation, is fully Trinitarian: no attribute belongs

---

12 "Thus the Trinity is the initial mystery, the Holy of Holies of the divine reality, the very life of the hidden God, the living God. Only poetry can evoke it, precisely because it celebrates and does not pretend to explain. All existence and all knowledge are posterior to the Trinity, and find in It their base." (V. Lossky; Orthodox Theology: an Introduction, p. 46. Crestwood, NY: St. Vladimir's Seminary Press, 1989.)

to any one of the divine Persons alone, but finds its unique expression in each of them.

Or rather, "attributes" is by far too academic and Scholastic a way of expressing the divine life for us: Eastern theology prefers to speak of the common life of the Trinity as the "divine names," or "energies," of God. "The divine names are the flow of the divine life whose source is the Father, shown to us by the Son, and communicated to us by the Spirit." (Lossky 1989, p. 48) The energies of God are the eternal radiance of God, uncreated energies, overflowing of the divine glory — grace, mercies, compassions.

The divine nature, which we call "essence" — God the Unknowable — and the divine radiance, which we call "energy" (Dynamis) — God the Knowable — are in the last sense, one nature. The divine energies while appearing in creation are in no way dependent upon creation. It is a forever radiance, in no way conditioned by the existence or non–existence of creation. (Lossky 1989, p. 49)

Nor do the divine energies "explain" God — Love, Wisdom, and so forth — for God cannot be reduced to the operations and manifestations of God in the created world, or even outside creation. No more than we can reduce God to creation, however much immanent in creation. God is more than the whole and the parts.

The Creation exists by the free will of God, and is other than God.

Creation is absolute, out of nothing, ex nihilo — a concept shared by Jews and Christians alone.

Creation did not involve pre–existent nature, or matter.

Creation did not involve "procession" from the nature or being of God.

Creation was ex nihilo, both as to matter and spirit — and as to will.

Creation is an activity of the Trinity: the very Symbol which we now discuss describes the Father as "creator of heaven and earth, and of all things, visible and invisible," calls the Son the one "by whom all things were made," and identifies the Holy Spirit as "the Lord, the Giver of Life."

Creator, like the other divine names (energies) posits each of the Trinity as being involved: the Father, as source of creation, working through the Son, in the Holy Spirit. Each creates, in a way unique and personal. In words that underline the phrase of the Symbol that we are now exploring –"and of all things, visible and invisible" — Basil says that the Father is "the primordial cause of everything that has been made," while describing the Son as the "operative cause" of things, and the Holy Spirit as the "perfecting cause."

AND IN ONE LORD, JESUS CHRIST

And in one Lord Jesus Christ, the Son of God, the Only-begotten, Begotten of the Father before all worlds, Light of Light, Very God of Very God, Begotten, not made; of one essence with the Father, by whom all things were made.

Christ alone is Lord. The head of the household (oikos), the one in whom the economy of salvation is proclaimed and realized.

To the dismay of the Roman Emperor, who had arrogated to himself as Imperator and Pontifex Maximus also the domestic title, "Dominus," the cry of "Christus Dominus!" ("Christ is Lord!") must have seemed subversive indeed.

But to the Household of faith, the point must have been obvious: there is only one community, one household — the household of God — and Christ alone is Lord there.

All things are delivered into his hands.

Christ is made "the heir of all things" (Hebrews 1:2), and "upholding all things by the word of his power (Hebrews 1:3).

"He is the image of the invisible God, the firstborn over all creation." (Colossians 1:15)

To the "Dominus et Deus" ("Lord and God") of the Roman emperor, the Church asserts but one Lord, Jesus Christ, to whom alone it says: "My Lord and my God."(Cochrane 1974)

> *Let this mind be in you which was also in Christ Jesus, who, being in the form of God, did not consider it robbery to be equal with God, but made Himself of no reputation, taking the form of a servant, and coming in the likeness of men. And being found in appearance as a man, He humbled Himself and became obedient to the point of death, even the death of the cross.*
>
> *Therefore God also has exalted Him and given Him the name, which is above every name, that at the name of Jesus every knee should bow, of those in heaven, and of those on earth, and of those under the earth, and that every tongue should confess that Jesus Christ is Lord, to the glory of God the Father.*
>
> Philippians 2:5–11 (NKJV)

THE SON OF GOD

If the Father is God-with-a-Son, the Son is God-with-a-Father. The scriptural testimony of Christ as Son of God is immense and constant. So, in coming to know this One with whom we walk on the divine and healing path, let us begin at the beginning, with the Gospel of Matthew, the third chapter:

> *In those days, John the Baptist came preaching in the wilderness of Judea, and saying: 'Repent, for the Kingdom of Heaven is at hand! "For this is he who was spoken of by the prophet Isaiah, saying: "The voice of one crying in the wilderness: Prepare the way of the Lord; make his paths straight."*
>
> Matthew 3:1–3 (NKJV)

Then Jesus came from Galilee to John at the Jordan, to be baptized by him, and John tried to prevent Him, saying: "I need to be baptized by You, and You are coming to me?" But Jesus answered and said to him: "Permit it to be so now, for thus it is fitting for us to fulfill all righteousness." Then he allowed Him. When He had been baptized, Jesus came up immediately from the water; and behold the heavens were opened to Him, and He saw the Spirit of God descending like a dove upon Him. And suddenly a voice came from heaven, saying: 'This is My beloved Son, in whom I am well pleased.'"

Matthew 3:13–17 (NKJV)

This witness of Heaven to the Son is a conflation of Psalm 2:7 and Isaiah 42:1, with reference to other passages in Isaiah. It is echoed almost precisely in Mark 1:11, and Luke 3:22.

I will declare the decree: The Lord has said to Me, "You are my Son, today I have begotten You."

Psalm 2:7 (NKJV)

Behold! My Servant whom I uphold, My Elect One in whom my soul delights! I have put My Spirit upon Him; He will bring forth justice to the Gentiles.[13]

Isaiah 42:1 (NKJV)

…The Lord has called Me from the womb; From the matrix of My mother He has made mention of My name.

Isaiah 49:1 (NKJV)

And He said to me, "You are My servant, O Israel, in

---

13 See also Isaiah 43:10, and 49:1, 3, 5–6.

whom I will be glorified."

Isaiah 49:3 (NKJV)

And now the Lord says, Who formed Me from the womb to be His Servant, to bring Jacob back to Him, so that Israel is gathered to Him... Indeed, He says: "It is too small a thing that You should be My Servant, to raise up the tribes of Jacob, and to restore the preserved ones of Israel; I will also give you as a light to the Gentiles, that You should be My salvation to the ends of the earth."

Isaiah 49:5-6 (NKJV)

Psalm 2:7 is echoed again in Hebrews 1:5, to which is added 2 Samuel 7:14, "I will be to Him a Father, and He shall be to Me a Son." –whose Kingdom shall be forever, and not taken away.

The Baptism of Christ is the opening of his public ministry. We celebrate it as the closing of the liturgical season of Christmas. In the East, we associate it with the Theophany,[14] for God in the Holy Trinity is present to us in that day: the Father, eternally begetting the Son; the Son, eternally begotten of the Father; and the Holy Spirit, eternally proceeding from the Father, bearing witness to the Son.

Baptism, as a passing through the waters, is marked in the Eastern Church by the blessing of homes at Theophany. Epiphany or Theophany is not only associated historically with the Baptism of Christ, but is the day on which the Nativity was anciently celebrated, quite aside from the "Three Kings," or Magi.

The Western Church celebrates Epiphany, and then the Baptism of the Lord following; so that the Monday next following becomes the first day in commons, or "ordinary time" — the First Week of Ordinary Time, in the liturgical calendar. Mostly, churches no longer mark the Sundays after Epiphany as in the

---

14 Also called The Epiphany

old Calendar.

If the Feast of the Circumcision (January 1) marks the participation of Jesus Christ in the Old Covenant, according to Moses, the Baptism marks the entry of Christ into the New Covenant, giving to the work of John the Immerser a new meaning, for Christ is now "the firstborn of many brethren" even as the ancient foreshadowings in the passage through the waters (at the Red Sea, at the Jordan, and in the waters of ritual and immersion) are brought forward.

In this, are the Son-ship of Christ and the Holy Trinity revealed together at the very outset.

And in this, is Baptism, as the mystery of our initiation into the community of faith and the divine life in Christ, established as the first Mystery (Sacrament) — at the very outset.

> But to the Son, He says: "Your throne, O God, is forever and ever; A scepter of righteousness is the scepter of Your kingdom You have loved righteousness and hated lawlessness; Therefore God, Your God, has anointed You with the oil of gladness more than Your companions."
>
> Hebrews 1:8–9 (NKJV)[15]

> And John bore witness, saying: "I saw the Spirit descending from heaven like a dove," and He remained upon Him. I did not know Him, but He who sent me to baptize with water said to me: "Upon whom you see the Spirit descending, and remaining upon Him, this is He who baptizes with the Holy Spirit. And I have seen and testified that this is the Son of God."
>
> John 1: 32–34 (NKJV)

---

15 Paul is quoting from Psalm 45:6, 7, and Isaiah 61:1, 3 as the author of Hebrews bears witness to Christ as Son

THE ONLY–BEGOTTEN

The one begotten. The Greek is very clear, for it is one word: monogenēs.[16] There is none other begotten of the Father. There is but one.

> *For to which of the angels did He ever say: "You are My Son, Today I have begotten You.?"*
>
> Hebrews 1:5 (NKJV)

> *Nor is there salvation in any other, for there is no other name under heaven given among men by which we must be saved.*
>
> Acts 4:12 (NKJV)

Even the Holy Spirit, proceeding from the Father, is not begotten.

BEGOTTEN BY THE FATHER BEFORE ALL WORLDS

Begotten by the Father before all ages (aeons).

Before Time was, and outside Time; before the creation was, and outside creation. For, if Christ was born in time, or in the first moment of creation, he is no longer God the uncreated, but a creature, however elevated and exalted a creature.

"Before" and "outside" really are absurd terms here, for they have no relevance to the internal life of the Trinity.

On a deeper level, Christ comes to us as the express image of God, the One in whom we see God, the One in whom we can come to know God (theology).

> *No one has seen God at any time. The only begotten Son, who is in the bosom of the Father, He has de-*

---

16 Monogenēs (μονογενὴς) is a Greek word that means either only child or only *legitimate* child.

clared Him.

John 1:18 (NKJV)

Jesus said to him, "I am the way, the truth, and the life. No one comes to the Father except through Me. If you had known Me, you would have known my Father also; and from now on you know Him and have seen Him."

Philip said to Him: "Lord, show us the Father, and it is sufficient for us?"

Jesus said to him, "Have I been with you so long, and you do not know Me, Philip? He who has seen me has seen the Father; so how can you say, 'Show us the Father?' "

John 14:6–9 (NKJV)

God, who at various times and in various ways spoke in times past to the fathers by the prophets, has in these last days spoken to us by His Son..., who being the brightness of His glory and the express image of His person...., sat down at the right hand of the Majesty on high.

Hebrews 1:1–3 (NKJV)

Christ Jesus is "the brightness of His glory" because he has his origin in the Father, and his nature is identical with that of the Father. And he is "the express image of His person" because as Son he is a distinct Person from his Father, he is an eternal icon (image) of the Father, perfect in every way. "Thus the personal distinction of God as Trinity is known only in the Lord Jesus Christ (see John 14:9). No one knows the Father but through the Son."(Gillquist, et al. 1993, p. 513, footnote)

There is no compromise. Having said Christ is the one and only begotten of the Father, the Church drives home the teaching of kerygma and Tradition (Scripture): that Christ is God, personal and incarnate. Christ is the Uncreated Light that springs from that Dweller in Light Inaccessible.

> *In Him was life, and the life was the light of men. And the light shines in the darkness, and the darkness, and the darkness did not comprehend it.*
>
> *There was a man sent from God, whose name was John. This man came for a witness to bear witness of the Light, that all through him might believe. He was not that Light, but was sent to bear witness of that Light. That was the true Light which gives light to every man who comes into the world.*"

John 1:4-9 (NKJV)

The Light which shines into our darkness is the light of Tabor, the light of the Transfiguration.

It is the light of deifying grace.[17]

VERY GOD OF VERY GOD

What comes of God is God. The Trinity is proclaimed clearly and unequivocally in the opening chapter of the Gospel according to John. Christ is the Word come into the world, Christ is light, and the light is life. And in Christ is the first and greatest of the theophanies (manifestations, revelations) of God:

> *For the law was given through Moses, but grace and*

---

17 "The distinction in God between 'essence' and 'energy' — the focal point of Palamite theology — is nothing but a way of saying that the transcendent God remains transcendent, as He also communicates Himself to humanity." (Meyendorff 1983, Introduction, p. 20)

truth came through Jesus Christ (Messiah). No one has seen God at any time. The only begotten Son, who is in the bosom of the Father, He has declared Him.

John 1:17–18 (NKJV)

As the chapter moves on, John bears witness as "the voice of one crying in the wilderness" to the Christ, and Jesus comes to the Jordan to be baptized of John — who testifies concerning the descent of the Holy Spirit upon Jesus ("I saw the Spirit descending from heaven like a dove…" John 1:32) and that this Jesus Messiah (Christ) is the one whom the Father had told John earlier "this is He who baptizes with the Holy Spirit." (John 1:33)

John's gospel (glad tidings) begins, as do the three "synoptic" gospels, with the revelation (theophany) of Jesus Christ at the Jordan, in the waters of baptism — which is at the same time, the revelation of the Trinity itself, and the beginning of the public ministry of the Lord.

This is not a teacher that has come to us, this is God.

In the beginning was the Word, and the Word was with God, and the Word was God. He was in the beginning with God. All things were made through Him, and without Him nothing was made that was made.

John 1:1-3 (NKJV)

BEGOTTEN NOT MADE

Christ is not a creature, or any sort of created thing, but is begotten of the Father before all things. The Father is now revealed, for there is a Son. And the Son is of the same nature and being as the Father, of whom he is generated, God. The creation follows, and is another matter altogether.

Most of the great heresies depended upon a refusal to acknowledge God as Father, and insisted that God had "sons" only in the earthly sense that we are all the sons of God; but we are sons only because there is a Son. Hence, many efforts were made, to explain away in one philosophical, rationalizing way or another, the fact of Jesus as the Word born of the Father before all creation began, Light from Light, God from God.

OF ONE ESSENCE WITH THE FATHER

Born of the Father, as a Son, the eternal Word shares the Father's essence (or, as the West says, substance). There is no distinction whatsoever in the essential nature of God, whether God knows himself as Father, or as Son. They are distinct as persons, they are one as God.

How else shall it be said that only the Son has seen the Father at any time, and that the Son is the perfect revelation (theophany) of the Father?

Ultimately, the Father and the Son are united in their one nature or essence with the Holy Spirit, and we come to experience the Three as One, Trinity of Persons, ever One God.

BY WHOM ALL THINGS WERE MADE

All things were made through Him, and without Him nothing was made that was made.

John 1:3 (NKJV)

God, who at various times and in different ways spoke in times past to the fathers by the prophets, has in these days spoken to us by His Son, whom He has appointed heir of all things, through whom also He made the worlds; who being the brightness of His glory and the express image of His person, and upholding all things by the word of His power, when He had by

*Himself purged our sins, sat down at the right hand of
the Majesty on high....*

Hebrews 1:1–3 (NKJV)

All of creation ("the worlds") came from the Father, through
Christ Jesus. In creation, the Trinity is present as a whole, each
person in a distinct way: the Father as Ground and First Principle, the Son as operative principle, and the Holy Spirit as effica-
cious principle. For, as with all the "divine names" or "energies"
of cataphatic theology (theology of light, or affirmative theology), each of the Trinity is present in a distinct way, but all three
together as God.

Christ the Word is the one who, begotten of the Father, and
the express image (icon) of his person, creates the cosmos and
sends the Spirit into it. (Ground, Unity and Diversity.)

*Who for us men and for our salvation came down
from heaven, and was incarnate of the Holy Spirit
and the Virgin Mary, and was made man; And was
crucified also for us under Pontius Pilate, and suffered
and was buried;*

*And the third day, He rose again, according to the
Scriptures; And ascended into heaven, and sits at the
right hand of the Father; And He shall come again
with glory to judge the quick and the dead, Whose
kingdom shall have no end.*

With these next sentences of the Symbol of Nicaea–Constantinople, we move from a discussion of who Christ is, to his saving mission: he came down from heaven to reveal God to us, and
to redeem the world as holy to God.

God made us in the beginning, as a free gratuitous act, and
God when we have fallen, raises us up.

In redemption, as in creation, the most holy and undivided
Trinity works, each person in a manner distinct: Christ comes

into the world obedient to the Father, and the Holy Spirit works to carry out the process by which the eternal Word takes on flesh and blood and bone, in the person of Jesus of Nazareth, the son of Joseph, the son of Mary.

Once again, the divine names — creator, redeemer — are about the Trinity as a whole, and about each person of the Trinity distinctly.

Once again, the human person is called upon to collaborate with God in the divine work, to become like God, in the divine and healing path. To walk and talk with God, and to work with God, to share a unity of love and experience. In this case, Mary, the mother of Jesus, Theotokos.[18]

WHO FOR US MEN

Men, here, means Man, the unity of male and female in one kind of being, as the Scriptures make plain:

> *And the Lord God formed man out of the dust of the ground, and breathed into his nostrils the breath of life; and man became a living being.*
>
> Genesis 2:7 (NKJV)

> *Then God said: "Let us create man in Our image, according to Our likeness."*
>
> Genesis 1:26 (NKJV)

> *So God created man in His own image; in the image of God He created him; male and female He created them.*
>
> Genesis 1:27 (NKJV)

---

18 The Greek (Θεοτόκος) title of the Blessed Virgin Mary. The word means "God-bearer."

Contrary to the dividers among us, the moderns so-called, who would like to present not one but two parallel human races, men and women, who have no ability to know one another, Scripture bears witness of one race of being only formed "in the image and likeness of God."

Contrary to the backward among us, too, the dignity of man and woman as expressions in the living world of the nature of God cannot be gainsaid, nor the inherent rights and destiny of that unified species being.

AND FOR OUR SALVATION

Our early parents in Eden were of a potential perfection, and they laid that perfection aside. In their sin, we became subject to all the rewards of that sin: death, disease, error, and all the other things that plague humankind.

C. S. Lewis

As C. S. Lewis says, in his wonderful story *Perelandra*, there was nothing that made our first parents subject to death until then, and their falling away from their destined perfection was in no way foretold or "in the cards." They chose. And they chose badly. The potential of Eden was lost, and they were cast out into another world, a world that must have seemed like a curse to them.

Genesis records God's words to the Serpent, to Eve, and to Adam, as three judgments or curses. (Genesis 3:14–19)

Yet, in the fullness of time, Christ came into the world, to restore Men to that original unity with God, and that original fellowship. In fact, over the centuries, God never ceased from pursuing His original will for us — and in that sense, in the constant movement of God's mercy, love and compassion toward us, we perceive our predestination.

The Church has often said that even had there been no Sin of Eden, even if Adam and Eve had not fallen from their first love and their potential for perfection, Christ would have come into the world. For, in time, it would have been necessary. But, once those evils had occurred, the divine mercy would not surrender what had been created, and Christ came into the world anyway, but worked differently that might have otherwise been the case.

The Lady in Perelandra makes it clear to Ransom that her destiny, and that of the King, are not as on his own world (Thulcandra, or Earth), for she and the King had met their Serpent — serpents, really — and emerged strengthened in their relationship to God, and their world emerges into its full self. Even as the Earth could have, but did not.

...CAME DOWN FROM HEAVEN, AND WAS INCARNATE OF THE HOLY SPIRIT AND THE VIRGIN MARY, AND WAS MADE MAN.

The Trinity is at work: the Father sends the Son into the world, this same Son by whom he created the world, and by the Holy Spirit is Mary made the Theotokos, the God–bearer.

Already, there is a shock to the sensibilities of the Hellenistic world, for the idea of God becoming material in any sense, or becoming human flesh, was repugnant to those who held "spirit" as holy and pure, and the material as impure.

Catholics know that all of creation is consecrated to God, and is holy. Contrary to Gnostics and others, Catholic Christians accepted the Incarnation (Taking on Flesh) by the Logos or Son, and expressed their acceptance of this union of material and spiritual, of human and divine, by genuflecting (or making prostrations) at these words of the Symbol of Nicaea–Constantinople. Yet, this world however holy in its inception had to be redeemed out of the hands of those into whose grasp it had fallen.

One symbol of this redemption was the consecration of the

Levites to the Lord, as his portion in Israel, who were to have nothing but him as their portion. As also the consecration of the firstborn male child to God, so that such children had to be redeemed by a Temple sacrifice. (Exodus 13:2, 12, 15; and Luke 2:23–24)

Catholics also express their love for Mary, who was a human being par excellence (Man), of an exceptional union with God in faith:

The Magnificat, her wonderful testimony to her cousin Elizabeth concerning the Angel's message, is a model of faith and acceptance of God's will for all of us. It shows a soul so in union with God, that there is neither disbelief nor hesitation when a visitation from Above occurs:

For as she had responded to the Angel saying: "Behold the handmaid of the Lord; be it done unto me according to your word." (Luke 1:38), her testimony to Elizabeth, the mother of John the Baptist, tells of a great and increasing love of God, and a conscious sense of who and what she represented in salvation history, a greater and greater unity with God in love and experience:

> *My soul magnifies the Lord,*
> *And my spirit rejoices in God my Savior,*
> *For He had regarded the lowliness of his handmaiden,*
> *For behold, henceforth all generations will call me blessed.*
> *For He who is mighty has done great things for me,*
> *And holy is His name.*
> *And His mercy is on those who fear Him*
> *From generation to generation.*
> *He has shown strength with His arm,*
> *He has scattered the proud in the imaginations of*

their hearts.

He has put down the mighty from their thrones.

And exalted the lowly.

He has filled the hungry with good things,

And the rich He has sent away empty.

He has helped His servant Israel,

In remembrance of his mercy,

As He spoke to our fathers,

To Abraham and his seed forever.

Luke 1:46–55 (NKJV)

Roman Catholics revere Mary as the Immaculate Conception, a teaching formalized by Pope Pius IX in 1854, and as the Mother of God.

The Immaculate Conception says that Mary, in view of her future role as Mother of the Redeemer, was from the time of her own conception the womb of her mother, Anna, preserved free of the effects of

Pope Pius IX (1792-1878)

Original Sin, and thus was all that Adam and Eve were created to be.

There are two problems with this concept, one political, and one conceptual. First, it is by no means clear that the early Church actually held such an idea as "Original Sin," in the sense that the Western Church has come to believe, and thus no basis would exist to consider Mary a special or unusual creature, however much we may venerate her memory and faith. Second, the Orthodox and others have never acceded to any concept of power residing in the Roman Pontiff that would allow him unilaterally to declare dogmas necessary to salvation, as Pius IX did in 1854, many years before the "primacy" and "infallibility" of the Roman Pope were proclaimed in the truncated and abortive "ecumenical council," Vatican I.[19] As the response of the Eastern Patriarchs at the time pointed out, they held no such concept of their own powers collectively as an ecumenical council, and had a different understanding of how the acts of an ecumenical council become ecumenical in fact for the Church.[20]

When Man sinned in Eden, the likeness of God was obscured radically, and the image of God in us is not always so easily discerned. Only redemption enables us to once again offer God (and the world) "fruits worthy of repentance."

As Martin Luther would have said, according to the National Catholic Almanac, "Man is radically — but not substantially — separated from God." To be sure, Luther shares much of the Nominalism of his time, and is rooted in the Medieval Scholasticism that the Western Church often used to express itself. Yet, Luther's point is like an arrow pointed directly at the heart of the matter.

The Sin of Eden subjected us to death, and to futility. And it left us to be born into a world of imperfection, capable of corruption. But not without help, and not without hope.

In a certain sense, the image of God in us — freedom, choice, and the like — can never really be destroyed in us, unless by the "sin against the Holy Spirit" we destroy the very basis of our capacity for grace, the reality of our being God's rational flock. The likeness of God in us — our moral likeness to Him — is often obscured, and not easily restored. Left to ourselves alone, we are

---

19 The Germans kidnapped Napolean III of France, and the French were providing cover for the pope during the Franco-Prussian War (1870-1871). Without the French soldiers, the Vatican's higher-ups went scampering. The initial act of the Second Vatican Council (1962-1965) was to formally end the first council.

20 As Bp. Elijah indicates, the Old Catholic Church rejects this teaching. That said, you are completely free to believe or not because all church adherents remain sovereign. Said another way: Christ came to take away our sins, not our minds.

hard put to even conceptualize the task, to understand what is to be done, and how.

What then, of Mary? Was she spared this human condition, in view of being Theotokos, God-bearer? Was she "immaculate" in the sense of the Roman Church? No, says Orthodoxy, she was as we are. But in her was grace, and grace abounding, even as it could be for any person who came into the world. She walked and talked with God, and was found worthy to be the Mother of the Redeemer. As the Angel said:

> *"Hail, full of grace! The Lord is with you. Blessed are you among women, and blessed is the fruit of your womb."*
>
> Luke 1:28 (NKJV)

*Theotokos icon
(History Museum,
Samokov, Bulgaria)*

Hail, grace–filled one! You were worthy to bear our Lord, and we proclaim your honor and venerate your memory, to all ages. Wherever the story is told, we rejoice in your faith and constancy, O Mary.

We are humbled by your humanity, O Mary, for you are Man as Man should be, and we desire to be like you, O most beloved Mother, able to respond to God's initiatives with a full and ready heart, a grateful heart.

For of you, by the Holy Spirit, the Word became flesh, becoming consubstantial with us, even as he is consubstantial with the Father, as God.

AND WAS CRUCIFIED FOR US UNDER PONTIUS PILATE, SUFFERED AND
WAS BURIED.

Christ came into the world to save sinners.

As John says: he himself is the Light that lightens all who
come into the world (cosmos), the Uncreated Light. But, even as
he came to his own, his own received him not. But to such as received him, he gave the power to become the sons and daughters
of God. (John 1:1–14)

It is not without reason that many churches had for a long
while the custom of the last Gospel, and some carry on that custom to this day. It is as direct an assertion of the Catholic faith
— over against those who would explain it away — as one could
wish. Like the ancient custom of genuflection or prostration before the words "and the Word became flesh," this reading of the
opening verses of the Gospel of John stood in the face of the
ancient Gnostics, and the theosophists and modernists of our
time — all the "Liquidationists"[21] of the Catholic faith — and
proclaimed the ancient faith anew, not only ancient but every
new.

> *For of His fullness have we all received, and grace for*
> *grace. For the law was given through Moses, but grace*
> *and truth through Jesus Christ.*
> John 1:16–17 (NKJV)

But, most of all, as Jesus himself would say later in another
way, having seen Jesus, we have seen the Father, for:

> *No one has seen God at any time. The only-begotten*
> *Son, who is in the bosom of the Father, He has de-*
> *clared him.*[22]
> John 1:18 (NKJV)

---

21 A perjorative term from Communism that means keeping government from
touching the economy, even to save it. The Marxists would say that the U.S. government was to blame for the Great Depression because they refused to intervene
to stop abuses of Wall Street speculation in the 1920s.

22 made him known

Cur Deus homo?[23] That Man might become God, respond the Alexandrine Fathers. Not that we enter into the wholly unknowable essence of God, but that we enter into the life (energies) of God. Deificatio (deification), theosis, and divinization are the terms that are sometimes used to express this mystery of our becoming godlike (godly).

And Christ could have done it no other way, given the recalcitrance of Man, but given also the freedom of Man. No deus ex machina[24] descending upon the stage of human history, setting all to rights and dispensing justice would ever suffice. But, God who is the Uncreated Light, descends to show us what he is, and what we are — and that is the whole point.

Legalistic concepts of sin and of redemption from sin do not address the essential issues. They cannot explain why Christ would have come into the world anyway, had Adam and Eve not sinned. As such, they are totally inadequate to carry us to the heart of the mystery, and hopelessly inadequate to express to us the depth of that love that should call forth our deepest gratitude and tears of bliss for the sheer glory of it.

Yes, we are taken out of our sins, and they are laid aside. For no other reason than that they are not and can never be the issue. They merely keep us from grace. It has rightly been said that when we come to God, the first gift we lay upon his altar is the whole baggage of our sins, and the burden of them.

They are no longer ours to bear, for we cannot. Rather, we turn away and leave them behind, and begin to walk in faith. Metanoia — a radical transformation of our body, mind and spirit has taken place, a mighty transformation. Not only that day, but every day of our lives. What God begins, he will bring to

---

23 "Why did God become man?" It was a common philosophical question back when seminarians studied Latin (and walked 10 kilometers uphill through the snow to get to class).

24 "God from the machine" in literature is a twist where the author lets some mythical thingy appear to save the heroes. Doctor Who's "sonic screwdriver" is such a device. Cinderella's fairy godmother could be another. This device tends to be frown on by uppity English professors and some publishers. (humph!)

perfection. Our conversion will be a lifelong process, as we walk and talk with God on the divine and healing path.

> *Therefore humble yourselves under the mighty hand of God, that He may exalt you in due time, casting all your cares upon Him, for He cares for you.*
>
> I Peter 5:6-7 (NKJV)

> *...for I know whom I have believed and am persuaded that He is able to keep that which I have committed to Him against that day.*
>
> II Timothy 1:12 (NKJV)

THE THIRD DAY, HE ROSE AGAIN, ACCORDING TO THE SCRIPTURES

Even when told, the Disciples did not grasp the teaching of the Scriptures concerning the Messiah. On the road to Emmaus,[25] after Jesus had died, two disciples walked along disconsolately, until the risen Lord joined them, and began to expound to them the meaning of the Scriptures, with reference to all that had passed. Yet, it was not until he broke bread with them that they recognized him. Are we much different today?

> *Now behold, two of them were traveling that same day to a village called Emmaus, which was about seven miles from Jerusalem. And they talked together of all these things that had happened. So it was, while they conversed and reasoned, that Jesus himself drew near and went with them. But their eyes were restrained, so that they did not know Him.*
>
> *And He said to them, "What kind of conversation is this that you have with one another as you walk and*

---

25 The town no longer exists. Archeologists say it was located about 7 miles north of Jerusalem.

are sad?"

Then the one whose name was Cleophas answered and said to Him, "Are you the only stranger in Jerusalem, and have you not known the things which happened there in these days?"

And He said to them: "What things?" And they said to Him, "The things concerning Jesus of Nazareth, who was a Prophet mighty in deed and word before God and all the people, and how the chief priests and our rulers delivered Him to be condemned to death, and crucified Him. But we were hoping that it was He who was going to redeem Israel. Indeed, besides all this, today is the third day since these things happened. Yes, and certain women of our company, who arrived at the tomb early, astonished us. When they did not find His body, they came saying that they had also seen a vision of angels who said He was alive. And certain of those who were with us went to the tomb and found it just as they had said: but Him they did not see."

Then He said to them, "O foolish ones, and slow of heart to believe all that the prophets have spoken! Ought not the Christ to have suffered these things and to have entered into His glory?" And beginning at Moses and all the Prophets, He expounded to them in all the Scriptures the things concerning Himself.

Luke 23:13-27 (NKJV)

We do not know why their eyes were blinded. Surely, it was a spiritual blindness. Yet, their hearts burn within them as he talked, and they finally recognize him in the breaking of the bread. Indeed, after such an exposition of God's work in Israel, how could they not?

Yet, they ought to have known, coming as they did from among those to whom the oracles of God were entrusted. To the Jews, it is said, the first Gospel, that of Matthew, was written.

For if one looks at Psalm 22 ("*My God, my god! Why have You forsaken me…*") and Matthew together, one perceives model and application, as Matthew expounds the ancient prophecies and applies them to the life of Jesus.

The Resurrection is the beginning of our faith, the central mystery, and in it we find the hope and the perseverance of the saints. For, if the grain of wheat falls to the ground, it shall rise again a new crop, and if we are buried with Christ, we shall rise with him to new life. This is the meaning of Baptism.

And it is the door to the next mystery: Pentecost. In Pentecost, the Spirit descends, and the transfiguring work of the Holy Trinity takes on a certain completion. At Pentecost, which we mark in the mystery of Chrismation, the Spirit descends upon the Disciples, and the Church becomes a living reality.

ASCENDED INTO HEAVEN, AND SITS ON THE RIGHT HAND OF THE FATHER

Christ ascends back to God, but as God and Man. And, as if to drive home the point, is seated at the right hand of the Father. He that is "Light from Light" and "True God of True God" is again in the heavenly place. But he that is ascended draws all things to himself, and in him is their hope.

HE SHALL COME AGAIN WITH GLORY TO JUDGE THE QUICK AND THE DEAD. WHOSE KINGDOM SHALL HAVE NO END.

We live in the "Last Days," the time between the First Advent, which we commemorate in the Eucharist, and "the Second and Glorious Advent, which is to come," as the Divine Liturgy proclaims.

We live in a present and real hope of the world to come. Indeed, we have already begun to live that reality, as we walk and talk with God. Our divinization, our *theosis*, is not put off, but it does not know its fullness until the time has come for that.

We do not know the day and the hour of God's appearing, nor the nature of it. We cannot know what transformation occurs when a new heaven and a new earth (cosmos) will appear, or what the process is. Even so, we cannot tell in what way the dead rise again, or what our new bodies will be like.

But we do know that we will reign with God, and the perfecting of our nature will be accomplished through the redemptive work of the Father, taken as a whole, through the Redemption in Christ Jesus, and the redemptive work of perfection (transfiguration) of the Holy Spirit, which creates in us, communicates to us a spirit that says to God, "Abba!"[26] and looks forward in eschatological hope in this world to the world that is to come ("Maranatha!").[27] Is this not witnessed by the very words of John, closing the Book of Revelation (Apocalypse), which itself closes the proclamation of the new Covenant (New Testament)?

> *He who testifies to these things says, 'Surely, I am*
> *coming quickly.' Amen. Even so, come, Lord Jesus.*
>
> Revelation 22:20 (NKJV)

And now we turn to the third Person of the Holy Trinity, the Holy Spirit, somewhat neglected among some Christians, but deeply loved and remembered among others. If Christ is our unity with the Father, and All in All, it is the Holy Spirit that is the diversity of gifts and communications in us.

> *And We believe in the Holy Spirit, the Lord and Giver*
> *of Life, Who proceeds from the Father, Who together*
> *with the Father and the Son is worshiped and glori-*
> *fied, Who spoke by the Prophets;*

The Church cleared its mind on the Holy Spirit at Constantinople, 381 A.D. Whatever doubts or confusions the Fathers may have had concerning the Holy Spirit were resolved there, and

---

26 A very informal word, similar to our "daddy."

27 Marantha (מרנא את) probably means "Our Lord has come." Early followers of Jesus used Marantha as a greeting

the temptation in the early Church toward a dyadic God (Father and Son) was lost in the full teaching of the Holy and Undivided Trinity (Father, Son and Holy Spirit).

WE BELIEVE IN THE HOLY SPIRIT, THE LORD AND GIVER OF LIFE

The co–creating Spirit, the co–redeeming Spirit, is Lord, and God. We acknowledge this, in the assembly of the faithful.

> *And the Spirit of God was hovering over the face of the waters.*
>
> Genesis 1:2 (NKJV)

> *Nevertheless I tell you the truth: it is to your advantage that I go away; for if I do not go away, the Helper with not come to you; but if I depart, I will send Him to you. And when He has come, He will convict the world of sin, and of righteousness, and of judgment:*
>
> - *Of sin, because they do not believe in Me;*
> - *Of righteousness, because I go to My Father, and you see Me no more;*
> - *Of judgment, because the ruler of this world is judged.*
>
> *I still have many things to say to you, but you cannot hear them now. However, when He, the Spirit of truth has come, He will guide you into all truth, for He will not speak of His own authority, but whatever He hears He will speak; and He will tell you things to come.*
>
> *He will glorify Me, for He will take of what is Mine and declare it to you.*
>
> *All things that the Father has are Mine. Therefore, I said that He will take of Mine and declare it unto*

you."

John 16:7-15 (NKJV)

*All authority has been given to Me in heaven and
on earth. Go therefore and make disciples of all the
nations, baptizing them in the name of the Father and
of the Son and of the Holy Spirit, teaching them to
observe all things that I have commanded you, and lo,
I am with you always, even to the end of the age.*

Matthew 28:19–20 (NKJV)

*Then Jesus said to them again, "Peace to you! As the
Father has sent Me, I also send you." And when He
had said this, He breathed upon them, and said to
them, "Receive the Holy Spirit. If you forgive the sins
of any, they are forgiven them; and if you retain the
sins of any, they are retained."*

John 20:21–23 (NKJV)

*But you shall receive power when the Holy Spirit has
come upon you; and you shall be witnesses to Me in
Jerusalem, and in all Judea and Samaria, and to the
end of the earth.*

Acts 1:8 (NKJV)

*Now when the Day of Pentecost had fully come, they
were all with one accord in one place. And suddenly, there came a sound from heaven, as of a rushing
mighty wind, and it fill the whole house where they
were sitting. Then there appeared to them divided
tongues, as of fire, and one sat upon each of them.
And they were all filled with the Holy Spirit, and
began to speak with other tongues, as the Spirit gave
them utterance.*

Acts 2:1-4 (NKJV)

WHO PROCEEDS FROM THE FATHER

Who has origin from the Father as from a single ground of God. The Western Church, beginning with sincere desire to refute certain heresies added here in the Latin, filioque,[28] which has become the source of many errors and disputes. Old Catholics, at Ütrecht, renounced the Western additions to the Symbol of Faith,[29] and in the recent period, Rome, without denying derived teachings, has authorized the use of the original wording by all Roman Catholics.

On one level, the matter is simple: ***no individual church official can add to the words of a Council***; and certainly it is generally acknowledged that the local and regional councils that first added the disputed words and others did so in good faith, and with good intent.

On another level, the matter is serious, going to the heart of Christian teaching concerning the Holy Trinity, and the Persons of God. Yet, ***the ancient teaching of the Church is clear: the Father alone is the ground of the godhead***, of whom the Son is begotten, from whom the Spirit proceeds. Thus, there is always only One God. But, also, our God is Personal: God comes to us as three Persons. The Spirit proceeds from the Father, and is sent on mission in the world (cosmos) by the Son — "of the Father, through the Son" says an ancient formula.

We cannot pretend to know the full economy of the Godhead, nor to know precisely what God is in essence; for, we know God only as the Persons of the Trinity, in God's operations or energies, not in essence. Let this be enough for us. But, let there be no confusions allowed to reign in the understanding of such of the mystery as has been given to us. And let us not introduce confusions.

God is not dyadic, a Duo, from which a Third proceeds; but

---

28 literally "and the son"

29 So did the entire Eastern church. By "Western additions," Bp. Elijah means the pope.

is a true and equal and consubstantial and eternal and essential Trinity. As the Liturgy says: "Let us love one another, that we may worship the Holy Trinity, one in essence and undivided."

Chrismation is the mystery of the Holy Spirit par excellence, sealing us in Pentecost, "the seal of the gift of the Holy Spirit." Baptism is our admission to the assembly of the faithful, and Chrismation is our pentecostal sealing, that we may in the Holy Eucharist receive the Body and Blood of Christ in Holy Communion, the mystery of our Oneness with him, and in him with one another.

WHO WITH THE FATHER AND THE SON TOGETHER IS WORSHIPED AND GLORIFIED,

The Holy Spirit, being God, is given the latria[30] and glory that is due God alone, even as are the Father and the Son.

Alone, and as Trinity, God is adored and glorified.

Holy God, Holy Mighty, Holy Immortal, have mercy upon us.

Holy God, Holy Mighty, Holy Immortal, have mercy upon us.

Holy God, Holy Mighty, Holy Immortal, have mercy upon us.

Glory be to the Father and to the Son and to the Holy Spirit, always: now and ever, and unto the ages of the ages.

Amen.

The Hymn of the Trisagion[31]

---

30 divine worship

31 A Greek word – Τρισάγιον – that means "thrice holy." This hymn is recited in Orthodox churches before the day's Epistle reading.

WHO SPOKE BY THE PROPHETS

All Scripture is of God, by inspiration of the Holy Spirit; and all prophecy comes from the teaching and the leading of the Spirit, for the good of the Church, for the building up of the Church.

Above all, as God has worked, the Spirit has borne witness. In the economy of salvation, the Spirit is at work, to teach and to prepare the way of the Lord, and to lead us into all truth.

In the Prophets, God the Holy Spirit gave witness to what was to come, so that we might know and understand. As we have seen, Christ held the Disciples responsible for knowing those prophecies, and taught them the fullness of what they did not know, did not understand, or (like Thomas) did not believe ("I believe, O Lord, help thou my unbelief." Mark 9:24).

May we with Thomas, say, in the Spirit: "My Lord and my God!" in the face of our Lord in the day of judging (John 20:28).

> *And We believe in One, Holy, Catholic and Apostolic Church. We acknowledge one Baptism for the remission of sins. We look for the Resurrection of the dead, and the Life of the world to come. Amen.*

WE BELIEVE IN ONE, HOLY, CATHOLIC AND APOSTOLIC CHURCH

"Old Catholic" as a name has had a number of uses, historically, and in the present day has often been rejected as confusing and divisive. However, our use of it is very clear, and very simple: Old Catholics are those who hold the ancient faith of Christ's one, holy, catholic and apostolic Church, as delivered once and for all to the Apostles, and handed down by them, to us.

The Old Catholic Church is the Church of Christ, pure and simple —

ONE

… because Christ is one, and the Church is the Body of

Christ, who is her head and high priest;

HOLY

… because God is holy, and dwells in her;

CATHOLIC

… because Christ is in her midst, and in Him is the fullness of truth;

APOSTOLIC

… because Christ delivered the worldly mission of the Church into the hands of His holy Apostles, and their successors in faith and practice, to this day.

The one, holy, catholic and apostolic Church of Christ witnesses to the world in her Tradition, which is nothing more or less than the living presence in her of the Holy Spirit, as she awaits the Second and Great Advent of our Lord and God and Savior, Jesus Christ.

The Tradition of the Church sometimes comes to us as kerygma, as Scripture, as the witness of her teachers and her saints.

The core teaching of the Catholic and Apostolic faith is set forth clearly in the Symbol of Nicaea (325 A.D.) and Constantinople (381 A.D.) — the Nicene Creed.

Together with the Apostles Creed, the Athanasian Creed, the Symbol of Nicaea–Constantinople provides an orientation to the ancient Catholic faith, held in one form or another by almost all of Christendom. All those baptized with a Trinitarian baptism and professing that ancient faith are Catholics.

On a deeper level, the Catholic faith received its fullest expression in what for lack of a better term we call the "Church of the Seven Councils." — since the common term, "the Undivided

Church," is somewhat a misnomer.

To be sure, the Church has grown in one or another of its parts since then, but there is a great reluctance on our part to acknowledge any universal and ecumenical action since the time of the last and Great Schism, around 1054 A.D.

We adhere to that ancient faith, and so are called "Old" and "Catholic," while we honor the presence of God among all the disciples of the several churches, and look for the unity of all that is in Christ Jesus.

We adhere to that Ancient Beauty, ever ancient and ever new, seeking the perfection of our love — even as the Blessed Augustine has said:

> *Late have I loved Thee,*
>
> *O thou Ancient Beauty —*
>
> *Ever ancient yet ever new —*
>
> *Late have I loved Thee.*

Yet, late or early, we are confident that our faith will not be disappointed, and we adhere to Him, and to Him alone, who is Christ and God.

> *O Christ our God, who are Yourself the fulfillment of the Law and the Prophets, who did Yourself fulfill all the dispensation of the Father: fill our hearts with joy and gladness, always: now and ever, and unto ages of ages. Amen.*

The Church is a mystery of unity with Christ, a communion of saints, his mystical Body. In the Church, we understand all who have gone before in the light of faith, and all those living with God in this life, here and now.

The mystery of the Church is a mystery of local and universal, of individual and community, of Man with God. There is no abstract "Church" apart from Christ and apart from the People; nor is there a universal Church that may ignore the local community. For, it is in the local Church that the whole Church subsists and finds its reality, while the local Church finds its reality in the greater communion on earth and in heaven, and is conformable to it.

> *"For where two or three are gathered in My name, I am there in the midst of them."*
>
> Matthew 18:20 (NKJV)

The Local Church, and her clergy and Bishop, may never be replaced or subjected; but they are in communion with God and all the saints, and with the earthly Church in the Holy Spirit. For it has been said, that Tradition governs the Church, which is the Body of Christ, but Tradition is nothing less than the indwelling Spirit leading and guiding us into all truth.

No abstract "universal" Church may seize upon the rights and dignity of the local church; but no abstract "local" Church may seize upon the holy things of the one, holy, catholic and apostolic Church of Christ. God is not mocked, and if the Church is Christ, and Tradition is the constant witness of the Spirit in her midst, let no one dare to twist or pervert the life of the Church in any way, or put any of her people to shame. It is to Christ we shall answer, and to the Spirit, and to the Eternal Father, from whom they take their being.

No one is a Christian alone. But let us not presume upon the life of the holy community, and its Risen Savior. Rather, let us seek and find there the fellowship of the saints, and the unity of love and experience that is the beginning of our life with God.

WE ACKNOWLEDGE ONE BAPTISM FOR THE REMISSION OF SINS

Baptism is our initiation into the community of faith, into the Congregation of the Lord (the Congregation of Israel, as it were). Like circumcision of the male under the old Covenant,[32] Baptism is the "mark" of the redeemed in Christ.

In Baptism, we die and rise again with Christ, and are made one with him, and all our sins are taken away in the waters of regeneration. We are made a member of the Church, the Body of Christ, the new Israel.

Baptism is not a mere ritual, however, but a divine mystery that uses the common element of water, and can never be repeated. The total immersion (triple immersion) in the waters of life is once and for all time.

Unlike the ritual baptisms or washings of the Old Testament,[33] the cleansing waters of Holy Baptism remove from us the effects of Eden, and admit us into the community of faith, making us capable in God's help, of "fruits worthy of repentance."

The Church here affirms, in this Symbol of Faith, that there is but one Baptism for the forgiveness of sins and entrance into the community of faith. As the Roman Church used to say, the sacrament of Baptism is "indelible" in the grace it imparts, and in its working. It cannot be repeated without sacrilege, by denying the validity of a true sacrament (mystery).

Baptism is accomplished as Christ commanded us, by running water, in which the catechumen is immersed three times, while invoking the Holy Trinity, Father, Son and Holy Spirit.

Historically, the Church in its holy Councils has rejected any baptism but a Trinitarian baptism as being a Christian baptism.

On the other hand, any person who has received a Trinitarian baptism is joined to Christ, and is directly or in some way connected to the Church of Christ. They are adherents or disciples, even when they are not in full communion with the Catholic Church. (North American Orthodox-[Roman] Catholic Theological Consultation 1999) Hence, when entering into full

---

32 Jewish law. The term means a contract between God and the Jewish people.

33 Christians refer to the first part of the Bible as the Old Testament. It is the holy scripture of Judaism.

communion, any baptized person is not "re-baptized."

Any person may baptize in emergency, although the regular clergy are expected to carry out the ritual under ordinary circumstances. All that is necessary is to immerse the person three times in running water, or pour running water over the person, in the name of the Father, and of the Son, and of the Holy Spirit, intending to do what Christ commanded us, or what the Church does. The common formula is:

> *I baptize you in the Name of the Father, and of the*
> *Son, and of the Holy Spirit.*

Western teaching allows that even an agnostic or an atheist or unbeliever may validly baptize in emergency by using water and the statement of baptism along the lines indicated above. All that is necessary is that such a person intend to do what the Church does, regardless of any personal status of belief or unbelief.

Why? Because in this mystery, as in all the sacraments or mysteries, it is the Holy Spirit at work to confect[34] the sacrament and realize the saving work. And God is faithful, to work and to complete the work in us that is begun.

There are many images of Baptism in the Old and New Testaments, from the Congregation of Israel passing through the waters at the Red Sea, and again led by Joshua at the Jordan, to the ritual washings of the Jews, and the Baptism of John the Immerser, the Forerunner — until the very Baptism of the Lord by John at the beginning of his public ministry. (Mark 1:1–11)

During the Holy Mass, the sprinkling of water during the Asperges[35] recalls our washing in the waters of Baptism, even as does the Lavabo of the later service. In the Eastern Church, the blessing of the home at Theophany (the Baptism of the Lord, Epiphany) is an annual custom. Many preparatory and vesting liturgies begin with a ritual washing reminiscent of our baptism, often associated with the ancient words: "I wash my hands

---

34 To create something by combining different materials or the authority to set rules.

35 ceremonial sprinkling of the congregation with Holy Water

among the innocent, and walk about your altar, O my God. You shall purge me with hyssop and I shall be clean; you shall wash me, and I shall be whiter than snow." (Psalm 51:7)

In Baptism, we fall and rise with Christ, and experience the whole mystery of the Resurrection.

WE LOOK FOR THE RESURRECTION FROM THE DEAD

If Christ came into this world to save sinners, and took on human flesh, then we are meant to die to our sins and rise to new life with him. "Why did God become man?" So that man might become God. Hence, we do not experience the Incarnation (taking on flesh) of the eternal Word without knowing at once that we dwell in the sure hope of his coming again, and the Resurrection of the dead. Our hope is in this world, and in the world to come.

> But if there is no resurrection of the dead, then Christ is not risen. And if Christ is not risen, then our preaching is vain, and your faith is also vain.

I Corinthians 15: 13–14 (NKJV)

> And if Christ is not risen, your faith is futile: you are still in your sins! Then also those who have fallen asleep in Christ have perished. If in this life only we have hope in Christ, we are of all men the most pitiable.

I Corinthians 15:17– 19 (NKJV)

> But now Christ is risen from the dead, and has become the first-fruits of those who have fallen asleep. For since by Man also came death, by Man also came the resurrection of the dead. For as in Adam all die, even so in Christ all shall be made alive.

> But each one in his own order: Christ the first-fruits,

afterward those who are Christ's at His coming. Then comes the end, when He delivers the kingdom to God the Father, when He puts an end to all rule and all authority and all power. For He must reign until He has put all enemies under His feet. The last enemy that will be destroyed is death.

For 'He has put all things under His feet.' But when He says 'all things are put under Him,' it is evident that He who put all things under Him is excepted. Now when all things are made subject to Him, then the Son Himself will also be subject to Him who put all things under Him, that God may be all in all.

I Corinthians 15:20–28 (NKJV)

Otherwise, what will they do who are baptized for the dead, if the dead do not rise at all? Why then are they baptized for the dead?

I Corinthians 15:29 (NKJV)

We shall be transfigured, and raised up in glory, and incorruptible. And so it is written, "The first man Adam became a living being.' The last Adam became a life-giving spirit."

I Corinthians 15:45 (NKJV)

And as we have borne the image of the man of dust, we shall also bear the image of the heavenly Man.

I Corinthians 15:49 (NKJV)

Death is swallowed up in victory.

I Corinthians 15:54 (NKJV)

As the Pascal Troparion[36] tells us:

> *Christ is risen from the dead, trampling down death by death, and upon those in the tomb bestowing life.*

Liturgy of St. John Chrysostom

AND THE LIFE OF THE WORLD TO COME

> *And I saw a new heaven and a new earth, for the first heaven and the first earth had passed away. Also there was no more sea. Then I, John, saw the holy city, New Jerusalem, coming down out of heaven from God, prepared as a bride adorned for her husband. And I heard a loud voice from heaven saying: "Behold, the tabernacle of God is with men, and He will dwell with them, and they shall be His people, and God himself with be with them and be their God."*

Revelation 21:1-3 (NKJV)

> *He who overcomes shall inherit all things, and I will be His God, and he shall be My son."*

Revelation 21:7 (NKJV)

> *But I saw no temple in it, for the Lord God Almighty and the Lamb are its temple. And the city had no need of the sun or of the moon to shine in it, for the glory of God illuminated it, and the Lamb is its light....*

Revelation 21:22–23 (NKJV)

> *They shall see His face, and His name shall be on their foreheads. And there shall be no night there. They need no lamp nor light of the sun, for the Lord God*

---

36 An Easter hymn in Eastern churches of the Byzantine Rite.

gives them light. And they shall reign forever and ever.

Revelation 22:4–5 (NKJV)

Even so, come, Lord Jesus! Maranatha!

How We Got Here

What a treat it was for me to let you read a piece from the late Bishop Elijah, the Old Catholic bishop of San Francisco, California. He is one of the reasons that I sat up and took notice of the Old Catholic Church. His writing made lights flip on: "Oh, that's what that means." He finally got things to make sense: things I had been taught by rote as a kid but never heard a good explanation.

It is partly my fault. I never whistled or raised my hand when somebody claimed that the pope was infallible. I should have said something like, "Excuse me, what the Sam Hill do you mean that there's this guy in Italy that God prevents from making errors." I probably would not have been happy with the explanation, but at least somebody would have tried.

The idea of papal infallibility is one of the main reasons we use a term like "Old Catholic." It was a precipitating event, as some of my college professors might have said. Others might say it was the "straw that broke the camel's back" if they couldn't find some original saying.

Papal infallibility holds that the bishop of Rome can speak ex cathedra (from the bishop's seat) and do so without error. To be fair, popes don't speak ex cathedra often. But when they do, Roman Catholics are supposed to sit up and pay really, really,

really close attention.

Members of the Orthodox churches think it is typically Roman (read: silly), and the concept of papal infallibility is relatively modern.

The first church councils were called by emperors and other civil authorities. No early church council was called by a member of the clergy, not even the bishop of Rome.

What's more, the actions of the first church councils were accepted as the rule of the church without requiring approval or ratification from anyone else: neither emperor nor bishop (or pope, who is merely the bishop of Rome).

There have only been seven Ecumenical Councils. A council is Ecumenical when it is truly universal: when bishops from every part of Christianity are invited and get an equal vote. The Ecumenical Councils are:

First Council of Nicaea (325) repudiated Arianism[37] and adopted the original Nicene Creed, fixed Easter date; recognized primacy of the jurisdictions of Rome, Alexandria and Antioch and granted the See of Jerusalem a special position of honor.

First Council of Constantinople (381) revised the Nicene Creed in regard to the Holy Spirit

Council of Ephesus (431) proclaimed the Virgin Mary as the Theotokos ("Birth-giver to God", "God-bearer", "Mother of God"), repudiated Pelagianism[38] and

---

37 A teaching that claimed God the Father created Jesus, but that Jesus was not divine.

38 A teaching that there was no original sin

reaffirmed the Nicene Creed.

Council of Chalcedon (451) repudiated the Eutychian doctrine of monophysitism,[39] adopted the Chalcedonian Creed, which described the hypostatic union of the two natures of Christ, human and divine. Reinstated those deposed in 449 and deposed Dioscorus of Alexandria. Elevation of the bishoprics of Constantinople and Jerusalem to the status of patriarchates.

Second Council of Constantinople (553) repudiated the Three Chapters as Nestorian,[40] condemned Origen of Alexandria, decreed the Theopaschite Formula.[41]

Third Council of Constantinople (680-681) repudiated Monothelitism[42] and Monoenergism.[43]

Second Council of Nicaea (787) restored the veneration of icons (condemned by some in 754) and repudiated iconoclasm.[44] This council is rejected by some Protestant denominations, which condemned the veneration of icons.

The take-away here is that theologians can't be trusted to come up with valid explanations of an infinite God while working with their finite little brains. On a good day, the church is full of holy people. Somedays, bishops and archbishops are about as helpful as an ashtray on a motorcycle.

---

39 A teaching that Jesus was born with a human nature that eventually morphed into a divine nature.

40 Nestorianism says that Christ has two natures (human and divine) but is actually two separate "persons." The mainstream church says that Christ has two natures but is one person.

41 The Theopaschite formula is Unus ex Trinitate passus est (meaning "One of the Trinity suffered in the flesh").

42 Monothelitism teaches that Jesus Christ had two natures but only one Will.

43 Monoenergism claims Christ had two natures, but tried to address Monophysite misgivings by the view that Christ had one "energy". The definition of the term "energy" was left deliberately vague.

44 Iconoclasm, Greek for "image-breaking", is the deliberate destruction within a culture of the culture's own religious icons and other symbols or monuments, usually for religious or political motives.

There was a running joke in seminary:

Q: Can you name the period of church history where church leaders came up with bizarre theories?

A: Thursday.

There is an old saying about hot dogs and other sausage: if you really like hot dogs, never go see how they are made.

If you are really interested in the church, avoid church councils at all costs! They are as bad as a hot dog factory. Bishops gather and debate tedious points of doctrine and issue documents that condemn others to the point that you want to hurl your linquini.

Even these seven Ecumenical Councils are not universally accepted today. Evangelical Protestants reject the Second Council of Nicaea, for example, because they reject the idea of icons.

The last church council that can lay any kind of claim at being ecumenical was in the year 787. Church groups continue to have meetings of bishops, and some even call them Ecumenical Councils. They are not: there is nothing ecumenical (universal) about a meeting that fails to include everyone. A better word might be synod, which is the meeting of bishops in a particular jurisdiction or denomination.

Old Catholics generally accept the work of these early councils because Christianity was unified.

Okay, back to papal infallibility. It ties-in nicely to the idea of a council.

First, the so-called Immaculate Conception is a teaching that the Theotokos (Blessed Virgin Mary) was born without the stain of Original Sin (the bad stuff done by Adam and Eve that got humanity thrown out of the Garden of Eden).

I know that I promised a discussion on infallibility, but the whole idea of the Immaculate Conception is a direct link to why the Roman sect believes so strongly in papal infallibility.

The Immaculate Conception was established as a Roman

Catholic feast by Pope Sixtus IV in the year 1476, and it is perfectly okay that he did this. Take it or leave it: members of the Roman Catholic Church were free to accept or ignore the concept and its feast.

Pope Sixtus IV (1414-1484)
(painting by Justus van Gent, Louvre Museum)

But it all changed in 1854, when Pope Pius IX declared that the Immaculate Conception was a dogma of the church. In a document called *Ineffabilis Deus*, the pope <u>ordered</u> Roman Catholics to accept the Immaculate Conception. He also said that he was making the pronouncement because he could speak without error on matters of church doctrine.

It is a circular bit of logic: a pope who was claiming to be speaking infallibility declared papal infallibility. If you drop breadcrumbs through the argument, it will take care of lunch because you will circle back around and find your own breadcrumbs before you reach the end of the argument.

Did you follow all that? A pope took an optional feast (the Immaculate Conception) and make it part of the church's core teaching (dogma) and required that all members accept the teaching. And he said he had the power to make such a declaration because he was also declaring that he could speak infallibly on church doctrine.

So one night in the 1850s, the church went poof: abracadabra: the bishop of Rome became infallible. The sweeping grandeur of the transaction is breathtakingly bodacious.

The First Council of Nicaea in 325 had declared that Rome was one of the major centers of Christianity and that the bishop of Rome was one of the patriarchs of the religion. That declaration from the Ecumenical Council fell way short of anything resembling infallibility for the pope or any of the other patriarchs (Rome, Alexandria, Antioch, Constantinople and Jerusalem). In fact the councils had ruled that Jerusalem and Constantinople were the lead patriarchs of the church. Rome, Alexandria and Antioch were secondary: important, but not the most important, and certainly not infallibly foremost.

When Pope Pius IX made his declaration in 1854, Roman bishops saw the circular logic the pope had created. They got together quickly to dot the I's and cross the T's. They met in what is called the First Vatican Council. This council, consisting of bishops loyal to Rome, met in 1868.

The council's proposed decree on papal infallibility wasn't popular with some bishops. The Italian bishops were not in the mood to listen to dissent, and there were far more Italian bishops than any other nationality. Most of the bishops from northern Europe and about half the bishops from the United States were so upset that they walked out of the council. When Rome reported the results, papal infallibility was approved by the First Vatican Council, and it was close to unanimous because those who were against the measure had gone home.

The council was not finished with its agenda when things got dicey all over Europe. Prussian armies invaded France and captured the French emperor, Napoleon III. In Rome, the bishops scattered as fast as they could. In fact, the First Vatican Council was never formally closed until a hundred years later!

Bishops who stormed out of the First Vatican Council in protest over the doctrine of papal infallibility approached the Catholics in the Netherlands and asked if they could hook up with them.

The Dutch said Sure, and the Old Catholic Church was born.

The Catholic Church in the Netherlands is the primitive national church. There's a story that the Roman patriarch commissioned Willibrord from England to head into Frisia (now part of the Netherlands) in the year 696[45] to evangelize the bumpkins of

---

45 Pope Sergius I (687-701)

the Northern lowlands. One of the things Willibrord found was a Christian Church already functioning. It had been founded by emissaries from France several years before the pope's envoy arrived.

That said, Willibrord is usually considered the one who founded the Christian church in the Netherlands. The headquarters of this national church has been in the city or Ütrecht ever since.

Throughout history, the larger groups (read: Rome) let the northern church run itself. The word "nether" (as in Netherlands) is a somewhat impolite reference to the hindquarters of livestock. You can say that the Netherlands is the kind of butt of the European continent, and the proper people of Italy and the refined people of France wanted no part of it.

When the Christians in the Netherlands needed a new bishop, the bishops in the main centers of Europe told them to elect their own and not to bother the important centers if Christianity.

The hindquarters (Netherlands) of Europe got used to taking care of themselves. Over the years, the patriarch in Rome put it in

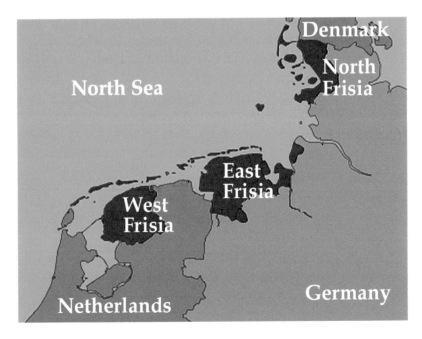

writing. In the year 1125, Pope Eugene III — at the request of the Emperor Conrad II of the Holy Roman Empire and Bishop Heribert of Ütrecht — re-affirmed the independence of the Dutch

church. This was later confirmed by the Roman synod called the Fourth Lateran Council in the year 1215.

It was not an experiment in democracy. Ütrecht is about 1630 kilometers (880 miles) by car, and they didn't have cars. They had a lousy cart with a horse. History might have been different if the Dutch bishops could have picked up the phone to call Rome or Paris or Jerusalem and made a request for a bishop. To get to Ütrecht from Rome, you had to get into your cart and coax the horse up through Italy, across Switzerland and the Alpine mountains. You had to negotiate the wilds of what is now Germany. And if you survived all that, you would arrive in the northern lands (a mushy lowland country that gets really cold). Switzerland is one thing, but the Italians never really forgot that the Germans helped bring down the Roman Empire.

Rome was the political force when Jesus was alive. Its reach included the Mediterranean areas from northern Africa all the way up to England. Christians knew their place in the Roman Empire, and it was mostly hiding from the authorities.

Eating the Body of Christ? Drinking His blood? The refined members of the Roman Empire were tolerant up to a point, but these Christians gave them the heebie-jeebies. It was disgusting.

All that changed when the Roman Emperor Constantine (272-337) declared that the empire was to be tolerant of all religions, including Christianity.[46] Constantine himself became a Christian late in life, but he made sure the empire itself was tolerant of non-Christians.

Constantine's mother, Helena, was an early convert. As the emperor's mom

Constantine and mommy (Helena)

goes, so goes the empire. It was suddenly quite fashionable to be Christian. Creeds were developed to make sure everyone knew it was not cannibalism to eat the Body of Christ. Church groups sprang up throughout the empire.

Christianity was not the "official religion" of the Roman Empire, but the lines between church and state were dimly drawn. To be a high-ranking official in the empire usually meant you were a Christian as well.

When the empire began its decline, there was a vacuum of authority. The church stepped in where civil authority once ruled. Europe was full of individual gangs under a knight or duke or prince, but the Roman Empire still existed in the form of its church.

The bishop of Rome stepped up and tried to bring unity to the chaos of the post-Empire period. He had his hands full: the French didn't like the Germans who didn't like the Spanish. The pope had his own army for the longest time.

When Islam popped up and overtook Jerusalem, the pope had about all he could stomach. Christian fighters were ordered

---

46 Edict of Milan in the year 313

to the Middle East to retake the land of Jesus.

And in the middle of all this, someone in the Netherlands said, "Hey, we're all out of bishops here. Could you send up a few?"

The answer was "Deal with it yourself. Can't you see I'm in the middle of a Crusade, for Pete's sake?"

And that is exactly what happened. The Dutch got in the habit of managing its own church. They had been doing so for hundreds of years anyway, but now the patriarch of the western church (i.e., the pope) made it official.

Rome made a mistake or two, of course. There was a matter of this monk in Germany. The Italians remained ticked at the Germans for what they helped do to the Roman Empire.

The monk in Germany was Martin Luther. He suggested that Rome had overstepped its bounds in 95 specific areas. Luther set

off a firestorm across Europe as country after country kicked the religious side of the Roman Empire back to Italy.

Protestantism in one form or another took hold in Germany, Switzerland, England, parts of France and Scandinavia (including Holland). Supposedly Luther just wanted some changes in the European church. What

Martin Luther (1483-1546) painting by Lucas Cranach

he got was collapse, like popping an over-filled balloon.

In the Netherlands, the Protestants were particularly harsh on anyone from the Roman church. That didn't include those Catholics around Ütrecht who had always been independent. The Protestants possibly thought something like, "These Catholics may be heathens, but at least they're our heathens."

Fast forward a couple of hundred years, and you will find that Europe has barely calmed down. Protestants hunted Catholics, and Catholics closed ranks. The Roman church followed its Crusades in the Middle East with an equally militant Inquisition in Spain.

In one case, some Spanish Jesuits were chasing a bishop named Peter Codde because they didn't like his theology. Codde made it to the Netherlands and asked the Catholics there for protection. Peter Codde was given sanctuary in 1704, and the Jesuits were sent packing.

This finally got Rome's attention. The Jesuits were tattle-tales! The Dutch had been running their own church for hundreds of years. Rome had said that was just fine, especially when you look at how impossible it is to get from Rome

Bishop Petrus Codde (1648-1710)

to the Netherlands (not to speak of the flat and mushy nothing you will find once you get there).

But tossing out the Jesuits? The pope excommunicated the Dutch bishops. The Dutch said that would be fine with them.

Rome also sent a new set of bishops to take over all the Dutch churches. This was less than fine, of course.

What followed were a hundred or so years of back-and-forth. The Dutch remained independent, and the Italian church continued to act like the official arm of a non-existent empire.

Travel and communication were still tough. The telegraph wasn't invented until the 1800s. Roads were unpaved, and train travel didn't appear until the 1800s.

Everyone in Europe was upset. As the Jesuits were chasing Peter Codde Europe was involved in the Seven Year War. Over in North America, the Yanks were tossing out the Brits in the Revolutionary War. The Holy Roman Empire, Great Britain, the Dutch Republic, Portugal, France and Spain were all involved in the War of Spanish Succession. This was only a few years after most of the European continent was embroiled in the War of

Austrian Succession.

With that setting, the pope was seriously annoyed when the Catholics in the lowlands of Northern Europe kicked out his Jesuits. The pope took back all the independence that Dutch Catholics had come to rely on. The North was to be strictly Italian in its religion.

And in the middle of all the angst and gnashing of teeth, up pops Pope Pius IX and declares himself infallible.

Troops were everywhere. Countries were armed beyond measure, and the pope decided to go out on a doctrinal limb and dangle red meat at the Germans.

The Germans, Austrians and Swiss Catholics all contacted the Dutch: "Hey, you guys have a spare church up there we can join?"

In fact they did, and the little independent and ancient Catholic Church of the Netherlands became known as the Old Catholic Church. The name was a direct slap at the Italians, who were creating novel innovations that were too much for the traditional-minded Germanic peoples.

This is only a few hundred years after the big Council of Trent, where the pope (Pius V) gave the world a new liturgy (the Tridentine Mass) and told everyone not to change so much as a comma or they would roast in hell.

Papal infallibility and the Immaculate Conception were larger than Pius's comma. The German states, Switzerland, Austria, Luxembourg and the Netherlands all bolted. They were joined by some in France and even Italy.

The Old Catholics got together and tried to make sense out of everything. There was no chance that they would ever reach consensus on the finer points of theology, so one of the first things they did is agree that each country is its own deal. You had the Old Catholic Church of Switzerland, the Old Catholic Church of Austria, and so forth. No official in one church could lay down doctrine for anyone in another church.

In 1874, they met in Bonn (Germany) and found there were

14 areas of agreement. In 1889, they got together and found 8 additional points of agreement.

In 1931, Old Catholic bishops met with members of the Anglican Communion and extended mutual recognition. An Anglican priest is interchangeable with an Old Catholic priest, so far as the Sacraments[47] are concerned.

In fact, there was a question on the validity of the Holy Orders of some Anglican priests. They asked Old Catholic bishops to come and conditionally ordain/consecrate Anglicans so that there would no longer be any question. The validity of Old Catholic ordinations (Apostolic Succession) is universally held to be valid, even by the Roman church.

The Old Catholic Church is not a Protestant church. It never broke away from anyone.

The Old Catholic Church is part of the One, Holy, Catholic and Apostolic church. If anything, the Italian church centered in Rome is the breakaway group.

The primitive Christian in the Netherlands (and all Old Catholic national churches) continues to pray for a reunion of Christianity. The fractures are annoying but not earth-shattering.

Old Catholics get along with many other religious groups: we're fine with members of the Anglican Communion and many others.

---

47 A sacrament, as defined in Hexam's *Concise Dictionary of Religion* is what Roman Catholics believe to be "a rite in which God is uniquely active." Augustine of Hippo defined a Christian sacrament as "a visible sign of an invisible reality." The Anglican *Book of Common Prayer* speaks of them as "an outward and visible sign of an inward and invisible Grace."

What We Believe

Church politics isn't pretty. It's fun (to me, at least) to watch bishops tear each other apart like livid cats in a burlap bag. Get me popcorn.

It is interesting – maybe important – to know how the Old Catholic Church came into being. It is the reasonable outcome of unreasonable clerics, doing the best they could with whatever information they had.

It's really interesting to note that the Old Catholic Church is actually older than its larger Roman counterpart. Old Catholics have been an identifiable group since the 690s in Frisia way up along the coast of the North Sea.

Roman theologians had been discussing changes to dogma since the time of Jesus. Some of the discussions annoyed the bishops of the east. Starting in the mid-400s, several popes refused to monkey with the foundations of the faith in the interest of unity. Then in the year 1053, Pope Leo IX "excommunicated" the entire Eastern Church after a theological argument.

Leo ordered "and the son" (filioque) inserted into the Nicene Creed. The eastern bishops balked (correctly). The pope left in a huff, which lasted almost a thousand years.

Part of me wants to laugh, but they were very serious about

the argument. And they are still serious about it: "and the son" is still an unfortunate addition to the Creed. Rome won't fix their crazy illogical tweak.

"Theotokos" and "Pantocrator" are fancy words. Maybe they are too fancy. The icons of the church can be gorgeous. Maybe they are too gorgeous.

Mary is the God-bearer.

Pantocrator mosaic
(Hagia Sophia, Istanbul, Turkey)

Jesus is the Almighty. It's what the words mean, but we have to make sure that the words don't get in the way of our marching orders. The artwork and architecture of our churches can't be allowed to insulate us from what we need to be doing.

> *For I was an hungred, and ye gave me meat: I was thirsty, and ye gave me drink: I was a stranger, and ye took me in: Naked, and ye clothed me: I was sick, and ye visited me: I was in prison, and ye came unto me.*
>
> Matthew 25:35-36 (KJV)

Fancy church goods are most likely from the church that Emperor Constantine would like. When we take those fancy things as more important than feeding the hungry, we're missing the point that Jesus tried to teach.

When Theotokos icons inspire deep contemplation, it's a wonderful thing. When they push us to working with the poor: that's Christianity.

God is everywhere, and that is why we can't see God. We only know about daylight because we have nighttime to use as a comparison. Day is not night: simple enough. But if we didn't have night, we wouldn't know about day.

Comparison is how our minds work. We have no "not-God" to use for comparison, so we cannot see God. There is no place where we can look that God isn't.

God is unchanging, and that is a difficult concept at first. We think everything changes. The universe expands. Things that are rock today will be dirt in a million years or so. Everything that is alive will eventually die.

Not everything we know changes: the number four doesn't grow up and become the number five. A four has been exactly the same as it always has been. Numbers don't decay or change. Numbers are not physical, which is why some philosophers have called mathematics a spiritual science.

The Three Foundations of Catholicism

The Catholic Church is based on three fundamental ideas: scripture, tradition and reason. Other churches, such as Protestants, define their spiritual experience more narrowly.

FOUNDATION STONE #1: SCRIPTURE

Some are **solo fides**, which means "only faith." Martin Luther was one of the first to say that people are reunited with God by the action of their faith alone. He would say that good works, such as feeding the poor, are important but don't offer "judicial pardon" for the crime of being a son of Adam and Eve.

More radical Fundamentalist or Evangelical Christians are in the sola scriptura camp. They say that Christianity is based only on what is written in the scriptures (i.e., the Bible). These Christians say that if something isn't in that book, then it isn't Christian. What's more, they say that every word of every part of

Psalmus, part of the Dead Sea Scrolls (c. 400BCE)

the Bible is without error.

Catholics in general — and Old Catholics in particular — teach that the Bible is the inspired word of God, but admit that it probably has a few errors. We feel that translators and people transcribing the words have most likely made errors over the past couple of thousand years. We don't want to "bet the farm" on any individual pen stroke.

What's more, Catholics would say that not all parts of the Bible carry equal importance. The first part of the Bible is called the Old Testament, the Jewish scripture. Catholics hold that the Old Testament is of less importance to Christians than the New Testament. Further, there are four gospels (Matthew, Mark, Luke and John) that cover the life of Jesus Christ, and we think these four books of the Bible are more important to Christians than the other parts of the New Testament, which mainly consist of letters between some of the earliest Christians.

Old Catholics would not scoff at anyone who believes their relationship with God is based only on their faith.

Some branches of Christianity consider themselves to be **solo scriptura**. They teach that the Bible contains everything you need to know. The book is infallible.

Old Catholics will tell you that (a) elevating ink spots on paper to the rank of an error-free representation of God is like creating a "graven image" before God; and (b) writing that has gone through as many scribes and translators as the Bible can't be blindly trusted.

FOUNDATION STONE #2: TRADITION

The second pillar of Catholicism is tradition, which is the unwritten word of God. Tradition is what comes to us from one generation to the next.

Tradition plays an important role in the ordination of our ministers. Every bishop in the Old Catholic Church maintains a document of Apostolic Succession, which is the bishop's personal lineage that reaches all the way back to one or more of the original apostles of Jesus himself.

Most Protestant denominations reject the necessity of Apostolic Succession, and no Old Catholic would say they are dooming themselves to the fires of hell. Nevertheless, for us, tradition is a critical part of our religious expression.

Only a bishop can ordain someone to be a deacon or priest, and all our bishops have unassailable and solid credentials that trace tradition all the way back to those who heard the very voice of Jesus.[48]

When a priest is consecrated as a new bishop, it takes three bishops to do so. That covers the case where there is some fault hidden in the past ("upstream") of one of the consecrators. When three bishops are present to lay hands on the new bishop, the chance of a break in the new bishop's Apostolic Succession are just about zero.

Tradition is what we believe. It is our responsibility to the next generation.

---

48 Even the Roman Catholic Church admits that the Apostolic Succession of the Old Catholic Church is golden, and they really don't like admitting such things in public. In the 1930s, bishops of the Church of England who worried about the validity of their own Apostolic Succession asked Old Catholic bishops to come and conditionally consecrate all their bishops. We were happy to cooperate with our Anglican brothers.

FOUNDATION STONE #3: REASON

The third and final leg on which our Catholic faith rests is reason. Said simply, Jesus came to take away our sins, not our minds.

The Old Catholic Church teaches nothing that we force on any member. That sounds wonderful. It is wonderful, but it is also deceptively simple. In practice, reason brings a whole host of problems.

I am personally pro-life. I am so pro-life that I take the position to its logical ends: I am also a life-long pacifist. If there is a war, you can take it to the bank that I'm against it personally. If a criminal is about to be put to death, you can assume that I am not in favor of that execution.

We have an ex-Marine in my home congregation, and he used to be in the military police. At home, he packs heat when there is a suspicious noise in the neighborhood. What am I supposed to do with that? Guns go against everything I personally believe.

His reasoning is as important to him, as my reasoning is important to me. With freedom comes responsibility.

If you come to me with the news that you a pro-choice, it is my job to let you be that way. The church stresses diversity.

*In necessariis unitas in dubiis liber-
tas, in omnibus caritas.*[49]

Rupertus Meldenius

*Rupertus Meldenius
(1582-1651)*

Unity in diversity is one of the most serious traits of the Old Catholic Church, and we are diverse! Here is an excerpt from our church law that tells members of our clergy to accept all kinds of people regardless of their personal beliefs:

> *I.05. (a) The Church encourages diversity. Although churches are legally exempt from civil rights laws, we do not discriminate. The following are not impediments to any Sacrament or ministry: citizenship, race, physical disability (including HIV status), ethnicity, family responsibilities, gender, gender identity, gender expression, marital status, national origin, physical appearance, political affiliation, sexual orientation, union membership or veteran status.*
>
> Canons of the North American Old Catholic Church

If you read through that list, you will find something objectionable, but we are all God's children. Each of us has the freedom of reason and the responsibility to let the next person have the same freedom.

And somehow it all works.

---

49 In essential things, unity. In dubious things, freedom. In all things, love.

Sin and Its Consequence

"Sin" is actually an old archery term. It means the shooter missed the mark.

Oops. Yes, we all sin. No, we're not all going to roast in hell.

There are several kinds of sin:

1. ORIGINAL SIN

Original Sin is what we inherited from Adam and Eve. They disobeyed God and got themselves (and all of humanity) expelled from the Garden of Eden.

Was there really someone named Adam, or is the story allegorical? Beats me. It is part of the Jewish part of the Bible, and I am Scandinavian, not Jewish. Original Sin, whether it exists or not, happened a long time ago.

What is absolutely real is this: if you live your life according to the principles set down by Jesus, you don't have to worry about any consequences from Original Sin.

Pay attention to the Eternal Now, and whatever Adam and Eve did will take care of itself.

2. ACTUAL SIN

Actual Sin is when you personally miss the mark. You did something you shouldn't have done (called "commission") or you didn't do something you should have done (called "omission"). You can't wiggle your way out of these kinds of sins by pointing your finger at poor Adam or Eve. It was YOU, missy, and you should be ashamed.

The Roman sect divides Actual Sin into two distinct classes of sin. I have never seen an Old Catholic teacher make a distinction, but you ought to know what the two classes are.

2.A. VENIAL SIN

The first kind of Actual Sin is a venial sin. This is your run-of-the-mill sin: lying, cheating, stealing, and so forth.

Jesus teaches you don't even have to take action on sin for it to be sinful. All you have to do is think about it.

Let me take a run at this teaching using New Age terminology. When you think about causing harm to someone, you are putting energy into the astral plane that gunks-up all your mystical machinery. That gunk attracts energy beings that feed on hatred, like maggots feed on rotting flesh. So these thoughts cause even more problems with the sender. If you send out negative energies, it ends up being thrown back your way thrice stronger.

Whatever: it isn't pretty.

All is not lost, of course. The church has a path back. You can be reconciled with God, the church, your neighbor and yourself through confession and absolution.

We are all involved in venial sin. It is part of being human.

Even absolution cannot give you full and absolute pardon on all levels. Confession and absolution can reconcile you with God and the church. It can set you back on a spiritual path, and that is incredibly important, but there are other toll takers.

Some would throw karma into the equation. You are free to do so under our diversity clause.

The civil authority may also be a stakeholder in the transaction. If you cheat on your taxes or murder someone, there is nothing that confession and absolution can do to free you from the debt you owe society.

It is all very messy. It is easier to avoid sin in the first place, but nobody seems to listen to that before-the-fact.

Mark Twain said that there are two kinds of education. The first kind is reading about carrying a cat home by the tail. The second kind of education, though, offers lessons unlikely to grow dim with time. If you actually carry a cat home by the tail, it is an education you will remember for a very long time.

2.b. Mortal Sin

The Roman church and some Protestants have a more profound class of sin, called a Mortal Sin. Pass the marshmallows: this is the term for a sin that will have your soul roasting in the fires of hell for all eternity.

A mortal sin is one that is serious, and you knew it was serious before you did it, and you pulled off the sin with the full intent of performing such a sin. The Romans say being an apostate[50] or performing an abortion are kinds of mortal sins.

We are now in an area that causes religious wars to break out. Here's an example: I am what you'd call a universalist. This is the personal belief that every person who ever lived will somehow reach the beatific vision (i.e., heaven). In other words, I don't personally think that God will send anyone to hell for all eternity. This is not an official Old Catholic teaching, by the way. Beats me how it will work: that's above my pay grade. But I sincerely believe it. It could be that we all get sent to a purgatory,[51] a place of soul cleansing where the gunk we caused during our lifetime is scrubbed off. Another possible mechanism is reincarnation: if we didn't get everything right this time, there's always next time. I am not in a position to tell God how to do His job. I am only in a position to tell you what I believe. My suspicion is that the mechanism is reincarnation, but that is just me. Reincarnation is not a teaching of the Old Catholic Church, and it is not something I would ever mention from a pulpit. It was taught by some early members of the Christian church. You are free to agree or disagree, but it is what I believe deep down inside.

What's more, I find such discussions invigorating. It is why one of my college degrees was philosophy.

The truth is that it isn't something you need to worry about. Is there a difference between mortal sin and venial sin? Don't

---

50 public denial of the faith

51 A teaching of the Roman Catholic Church, but their purgatory cleanses souls only of venial sins. Those who die with a mortal sin on their scorecard do not pass go or collect $200. They go straight into hell for all eternity.

worry about it: follow the teaching of Jesus, and that teaching will take care of all your sin.

Sin misses the mark. *Honest soul-searching is the only fool-proof way of identifying your sins.* Preparing for confession is like making a personal inventory: both good and bad.

Jesus Christ died on the cross. He descended into hell, and he did this so you don't have to. He rose from the dead to bring you the good news of salvation. It was like someone with great authority said, "Here, do it this way."

THE THREE THEOLOGICAL VIRTUES

A virtue is being righteous or good. A theological virtue is being morally good and in focus with God.

FAITH

> *"Blessed are those who have not seen and yet have believed."*
>
> John 20:29 (NKJV)

Faith is when you know something to be true even if you are not able to see it.

Faith happens all the time. You have faith that there is the number three, but you have never seen the number three. You can see three apples or three guitar strings, but you have never actually seen the number three itself.

Faith is actually more than a simple belief. "Belief" comes to us from Scandinavia, where "lief" means hope, and "be" is put onto the front of a word to mean "lots and lots." So belief happens when you are overrun with hope.

Faith is when you know without seeing. A saying popular in

Alcoholics Anonymous is "Expect a Miracle." It doesn't tell its members to hope that some miracle will occur. It says to expect it, and thousands will tell you that their recovery from addiction was miraculous. It happens with enough frequency that members have come to expect it. That's faith, not belief.

HOPE

Hope involves trust. When you say you trust in God, it is an expression of hope.

The Lord's Prayer is a famous passage in which Jesus gives us a few things to pray for. Close to the top is "give us this day our daily bread." It doesn't say to pray for next week's bread, not next month's paycheck. It tells us to pull ourselves back to the day at hand. When we pray for our daily bread, it implies that we place our hope in God that He will be there for us next week and next month.

The hardest part about hope is actually trying it. The first thing that happens when we try to pull ourselves back to the Eternal Now is that little voice inside that says, "Your world is going to fall apart if you don't plan for tomorrow."

Most of us have never gotten past that little voice. Most of us have never let go enough to show deep hope in God. Jesus says, "Oh, ye of little faith," and he means that we are so consumed with worry about tomorrow that we lose hope. He was very clear: pray for our *daily* bread. Trust God for tomorrow.

CHARITY

> But when the Pharisees heard that He had silenced the Sadducees, they gathered together. Then one of them, a lawyer, asked Him a question, testing Him, and saying, "Teacher, which is the great commandment in the law?"
>
> Jesus said to him, "'You shall love the LORD your God

*with all your heart, with all your soul, and with all
your mind.' This is the first and great commandment.
And the second is like it: 'You shall love your neighbor
as yourself.' On these two commandments hang all the
Law and the Prophets."*

Matthew 22:34-40 (NKJV)

*"You have heard that it was said, 'You shall love your
neighbor and hate your enemy.' But I say to you, love
your enemies, bless those who curse you, do good to
those who hate you, and pray for those who spitefully
use you and persecute you, that you may be sons of
your Father in heaven; for He makes His sun rise on
the evil and on the good, and sends rain on the just
and on the unjust. For if you love those who love you,
what reward have you? Do not even the tax collectors
do the same? And if you greet your brethren only,
what do you do more than others? Do not even the
tax collectors do so? Therefore you shall be perfect,
just as your Father in heaven is perfect.*

Matthew 5:43-48 (NKJV)

This is where Christianity gets difficult. The rule sounds
good, but it is absolutely the hardest thing to pull off.

Love God, love yourself, and love your neighbor. Check.

But love your enemy? Oy.

Make the list: God: check. Spouse: check. Kids: not today...
okay, check. Sweet little Johnny next door who crushed a sprin-
kler head in the front yard and cost me $50 and half of a Saturday
to repair: Grrrr... check.

Then it gets really tough for me. I'm supposed to love hateful
right-wing politicians. I'm supposed to love the lethal followers
of Al Qaeda.

If a hospital called to find a priest because a lying pedophile
priest was in an accident and was requesting Last Rites, what

would I do? Say it is the same priest who made life pure hell for the LGBT kids in that priest's parish. If a famous neo-Nazi skinhead called and said he wanted to be baptized, what would I do?

I know what I'm supposed to do. If anyone reaches out, it is the duty of a priest or bishop to be there. I have looked through church law for a loophole, but there isn't one. It doesn't say that I have to like the person. I'm supposed to love them.

You can love someone without liking them.

Oh, and you don't have to know all the details to love them. That's called "dispassionate love" in the trade. If you ask for a blessing, I don't need your entire life story in order to perform the blessing. It is often better that I don't know everything. You already know that I am a life-long pacifist, so if you get me into a debate about warfare, there's going to be trouble. (As a philosophy major, I know all the little nooks and crannies of where a warmonger will run to hide, and I will win that debate, leaving you squealing for help. We don't need that.)

Charity means love, but it is the kind of love that involves kindness and tolerance. It isn't the kind of love that leads to marriage, and it isn't the kind of love you feel for your parents or siblings.

I don't have to know anything about you in order to be charitable towards you. If you ask for assistance, I need to be there. If you need a shoulder to cry on, I need to show you compassion. If you find yourself backed into a corner, I need to be understanding. If you are hurting, I need to be there with empathy or sympathy or goodwill.

On a good day, I can do this in my sleep. On a bad day, it takes every bit of God's grace from snapping your head off. I have lots of rape-and-pillage Viking blood in my veins, and I am a work-in-progress, you see. My main goal is to be better at charity today than I was yesterday. I seek progress, not perfection.

The good news is that I don't have to deal with either Al Qaeda today! That's good for them, and it is good for me. I wonder which would stretch my charity the most....

Though I speak with the tongues of men and of angels, but have not love, I have become sounding brass or a clanging cymbal. And though I have the gift of prophecy, and understand all mysteries and all knowledge, and though I have all faith, so that I could remove mountains, but have not love, I am nothing. And though I bestow all my goods to feed the poor, and though I give my body to be burned, but have not love, it profits me nothing.

Love suffers long and is kind; love does not envy; love does not parade itself, is not puffed up; does not behave rudely, does not seek its own, is not provoked, thinks no evil; does not rejoice in iniquity, but rejoices in the truth; bears all things, believes all things, hopes all things, endures all things.

Love never fails. But whether there are prophecies, they will fail; whether there are tongues, they will cease; whether there is knowledge, it will vanish away. For we know in part and we prophesy in part. But when that which is perfect has come, then that which is in part will be done away.

When I was a child, I spoke as a child, I understood as a child, I thought as a child; but when I became a man, I put away childish things. For now we see in a mirror, dimly, but then face to face. Now I know in part, but then I shall know just as I also am known.

And now abide faith, hope, love, these three; but the greatest of these is love.

I Corinthians 13:1-13 (NKJV)

The Gifts of the Holy Spirit

The Holy Spirit is God, one of the three persons of the Trinity. Some say the Holy Spirit is Sophia, the feminine aspect of God. The Holy Spirit (spiritus sanctus in Latin) first appeared after the crucifixion, after the resurrection of Jesus.

When Jesus ascended into heaven, the Holy Spirit descended onto the remaining apostles. We mark this event with the festival called Pentecost, one of the great feasts of the church calendar.

The Holy Spirit is what fills us with God's grace today. Whether the spirit is masculine (as it is in Latin) or feminine (as it is in the original Greek), it is the Person of God that is here and sticks to the skin. It isn't some remote theory: we encounter the Holy Spirit every day.

Tradition tells us that the Holy Spirit comes laden with seven gifts:

1. wisdom
2. understanding
3. counsel
4. fortitude
5. knowledge
6. piety
7. awe

The word "awe" is often translated into the English word "fear," but a better word would be respect. Throughout the Jewish scripture, we read about a God with his expectations and a terrible temper. The Christian part of the Bible shows God as more loving. When an angel appears, it usually starts the conversation with "Don't be afraid…." So fear is not what comes from the God of the Christian Bible.

The promise of God is that you don't have to face life by yourself. You have a built-in support mechanism. In addition to the church, you have the gifts of the Holy Spirit. When you fill yourself with faith and hope and charity, these gifts will be there. That's God's promise, and you can take it to the bank.

The Sacraments

A sacrament is "a rite in which God is uniquely active."(Hexham) It is "an outward and visible sign of an inward and invisible Grace." (*Book of Common Prayer* 1928)

Most Christian denominations accept some sacraments, even if they don't use the term.

Catholics are taught there are seven sacraments, and they were all instituted by Jesus Christ himself: Baptism, Confirmation, Eucharist, Holy Orders, Matrimony, Absolution and Unction.

THE THREE THINGS REQUIRED FOR EVERY SACRAMENT

A Sacrament is effective when done the right way. There are always three things associated with a sacrament:

1. **Form** is the liturgy used.
2. **Matter** involves the physical tools or implements.
3. **Intent** is the mind-set of the minister.

When you have all three of these components, you have a valid Sacrament. If you are missing one, it isn't a sacrament. In the following pages, you will find out how form, matter and intent are involved in each of the seven Sacraments.

The Blessed Sacrament

THE EUCHARIST

> *For I received from the Lord that which I also delivered to you: that the Lord Jesus on the same night in which He was betrayed took bread; and when He had given thanks, He broke it and said, "Take, eat; this is My body which is broken for you; do this in remembrance of Me."*
>
> I Corinthians 11:23-34 (NKJV)

> *Then He took the cup, and when He had given thanks He gave it to them, and they all drank from it. And He said to them, "This is My blood of the new covenant, which is shed for many."*
>
> Mark 14:23-24 (NKJV)

Almost all Christian denominations celebrate the Lord's Supper in one way or another. Some consider it nothing more than a memorial, not a sacrament that conveys God's Grace.

The Eucharist[52] recreates the last meal shared by Jesus and his closest apostles. The liturgy itself can also be called the Eucharist. More often, Catholics call the liturgy the Mass,[53] while our brothers and sisters in the East prefer the term Divine Liturgy.

The Eucharist can refer to the liturgy or to the elements (bread and wine) used in the liturgy. One of the biggest differences between Catholics and most Protestants is that Catholic say that the bread becomes the actual essence of the Body of Christ, and

---

52 The word comes from the Ancient Greek word εὐχαριστία (eucharistia), which means gratitude or thankfulness.

53 The word Mass is the source of some really fun arguments in seminary. It either comes from the Latin word for "table" or the Latin word for "send." I think it comes from "table" but I can argue the other side in a pinch.

the wine becomes the actual essence of the Blood of Christ.

Members of the Roman sect define how this happens: transubstantiation, which is one of those philosophical terms of more interest to theologians than the typical lay person. It means the essence of the element is changed forever, while the appearance remains untouched. The bread will still taste like bread, but its essence[54] is changed.

Old Catholics believe that Christ's real presence is in both the bread and wine, but defining the mechanism is above our pay grade. It may very well be transubstantiation. However it happens, we know that the transformation does happen.

All Christians agree on one thing: we are supposed to repeat the sharing of bread and wine because that is what Jesus told us to do:

> When you do these things, do this in memory of me.
>
> Knott Liturgy

Altar bread technically is made from wheat flour and water and nothing else. In the Roman church, if you can't take gluten, you are just out of luck. Most Old Catholic priests will try to find some accommodation for allergies (within reason). No, you can't do Communion with chocolate cookies. Yes, someone really requested that.

What "these things" mean is the subject of many religious fights. A Baptist will tell you that anything more than a simple memorial is too gruesome for words. A Roman Catholic will tell you that not only are you to be at the celebration of the Mass, you are required to take Holy Communion at least once a year.

Some of the greatest music and writing is on the subject of the Eucharist. *Panis Angelicus* is one example. The words were

---

54 fundamental nature

written by Thomas Aquinas (1225-1274). Set to music by several, but the version by César Franck (1822-1890) is one of the great compositions of all time.

Bread of Angels,	*Panis angelicus*
made the bread of men;	*fit panis hominum;*
The Bread of heaven	*Dat panis cœlicus*
puts an end to all symbols:	*figuris terminum:*
A thing wonderful!	*O res mirabilis!*
The Lord becomes our food:	*manducat Dominum*
poor, a servant, and humble.	*Pauper, servus, et humilis.*
We beseech Thee,	*Te trina Deitas*
Godhead One in Three	*unaque poscimus:*
That Thou wilt visit us,	*Sic nos tu visita,*
as we worship Thee,	*sicut te colimus;*
lead us through Thy ways,	*Per tuas semitas*
We who wish to reach the light	*duc nos quo tendimus,*
in which Thou dwellest.	*Ad lucem quam inhabitas.*
Amen.	*Amen.*

My favorite hymn ever written is about the Eucharist. It is by Mozart. The lyrics for *Ave Verum Corpus* come from the fourteenth century, supposedly written by Pope Innocent VI (1295-1362). Although they were put to music by many, the version by Wolfgang Amadeus Mozart (1756-1791) simply have no parallel in human history. Music just doesn't get better than Mozart's *Ave Verum Corpus*. It makes my heart soar every time I hear it, whether coming from the strength of a baritone like Bryn Terfel of Wales to the angelic soprano voices of the Texas Boys' Choir.

Hail, true body	*Ave, verum corpus*
born of the Virgin Mary,	*natum de Maria Virgine,*
Who truly suffered, sacrificed	*Vere passum immolatum*
on the Cross for man,	*in Cruce pro homine,*
Whose pierced side over-	*Cujus latus perforatum*
flowed	*unda fluxit (et) sanguine,*
with [water] and blood,	*Esto nobis praegustatum*
Be for us a foretaste	*in mortis examine.*
In the test of death.	

We sing *Ave Verum Corpus* at my home church sometimes. I put it up on the hymn board. It isn't complicated, but Mozart sort of demands rehearsals and practice, possibly professional singers. It doesn't matter. Even the unskilled chorus of a small congregation that doesn't know beans about Latin brings me to tears every time (very embarrassing for a tough Viking like me).

The Eucharist is called the Blessed Sacrament, and so it is.

FORM

If the meaning of the Eucharist causes Christians to fight amongst themselves, its form is just as big a source of consternation. Should we celebrate the Mass in Latin, Greek, Aramaic[55] or the local language?

The Mass is a kind of liturgical fire hydrant, with all kinds of church leaders trying to leave their mark.

One thing is certain: the form of the Mass changes. What you may not know is that the basic structure of the Mass has been fairly stable since the year 800 (roughly). If knights from the Crusades could be transported to the 21st Century, they would be able to follow along with the Mass even if they don't under-

---

55 Aramaic is the Hebrew'esque language spoken by Jesus. It is to Hebrew as Yiddish is to German. I think if you put a bunch of hot marbles in your mouth and speak Hebrew, what comes out will be Aramaic.

stand the words.

In the Eastern Church, the form of the Mass is the Divine Liturgy, commonly the one attributed to John Chrysostom. In the Western Church, bishops had quite a bit of flexibility. For a thousand years, the specific rules (rubrics) for saying Mass and its words were a little different depending on where you were.

*Pope Pius V
painting by el Greco*

That flexibility came to a screeching halt in the 1550s when Rome's Council of Trent established the so-called Tridentine Mass as the official liturgy of the church. Pope Pius V (1504-1572) said nobody would ever be allowed to change so much as a comma in the Mass.

That lasted until later popes found ways to "improve" the liturgy. Pope John XXIII (1881-1963) tweaked the list of saints and got rid of the "second confession." Pope Paul VI (1897-1978) turned the altar around, banished Latin, threw out the baby and the bath water.

The North American Old Catholic Church has two official liturgies: the Latin Mass (typical of 1958, i.e., before Pope John XXIII started tweaking things) and the Knott Mass (an English translation closely following the older Latin Mass). But the Old Catholic Church goes back to the older practice of giving bishops a bit of space to make decisions on other forms of the Mass. For example, we have a priest who says Mass inside a nursing home, and all of the attendees are most familiar with the Mass of Paul VI, so that is the liturgy he uses.

The sine qua non[56] form is a validly ordained priest looking at the Host (bread) and repeating Christ's words ("This is my body" or "Hoc est enim Corpus Meum.") in some language, followed by that priest looking at wine in the chalice and repeating

---

56 without which, nothing

Christ's words ("This is the cup/chalice of my blood"). Those are the "must have" items in every Mass.

Our celebration of the Mass tends to be very old fashioned, but there is a bit of flexibility.

MATTER

The Matter in the Mass refers to the bread and wine. The bread is officially unleavened wheat, made from wheat and water and nothing else. If there is a pastoral reason — such as a priest or congregant who is allergic to all forms of wheat — a bishop can make an exception. Yeast bread is never used.

The wine is the fruit of the grape. In most cases, it really is wine. Some priests who are members of Alcoholics Anonymous use an unfermented wine, while other who want to protect against the spread of germs use a fortified wine (sherry and other wines are spiked with distilled spirit to raise their alcohol content, thereby killing more germs).

Again, the Old Catholic Church tries to strike a balance of tradition with common sense. You can't waltz in with chocolate bread and try to say Mass, but you might use Hosts made of rice flour and water if there's a good reason to do so.

INTENT

The priest who says Mass must have the intent of causing the bread to be changed into the Body of Christ and the wine to be changed into the Blood of Christ.

This intent is not something you can observe from the pews. You have to take the priest's intent as part of your faith.

By the way, bishops don't say Mass! That may be seem strange at first read, but it is absolutely true.

When a bishop or archbishop is the celebrant at Mass, he or

she begins the liturgy wearing a zucchetto, which is fuchsia for bishops and scarlet for archbishops. He or she also wears an episcopal ring, often with an amethyst for bishops and a sapphire for archbishops. Both the zucchetto and ring are symbols of the bishop's jurisdiction.

Watch what happens during the Mass. At the start of the Canon (the section where the bread and wine are consecrated), a server will come behind the bishop or archbishop and remove the zucchetto. Sometimes the bishop does this without the server.

zucchetto in "bishop's purple" (magenta)

During the actual consecration, no bishop wears any symbol of jurisdiction: no zucchetto, no episcopal ring. It happens quickly and without great ceremony, but the bishop always "demotes" himself or herself from the start of the Canon through the end of Communion. The consecration is done by a priest, and all bishops continue to be priests even if they are given additional duties due to their office.

The Rites of Passage

BAPTISM

The word baptism comes from the Greek word that means to immerse or to wash.

Ritual cleansing in religion isn't new. Egyptian priests were some of the cleanest humans ever to walk the earth. They performed ritual bathing several times each day.

Today, Christians consider Baptism to be the Rite of Initiation. It is the liturgy performed when someone joins the Catholic

Church.

Some denominations require total immersion in a river or large tank of water. Old Catholics are okay with this, but we more commonly pour water on the new Catholic.

A few denominations — such as Quakers and the Salvation Army — don't see baptism as necessary. Roman Catholics say it is absolutely critical for salvation, and without it you are destined to hell. Romans then had to invent "baptism by blood" for their martyrs who were killed before being baptized and "baptism by desire" to cover those who die while studying to be baptized.

Baptism can get really complicated, especially when you get bureaucrats and philosophy majors involved. Archbishops are all bureaucrats, and one of my undergraduate degrees is in philosophy, so it is the classic Double Whammy. I can complicate this thing beyond recognition, but the rules of the Old Catholic Church tell me to sit down and be quiet.

As usual, the Old Catholic Church tries to offer a balanced approach. Yes, Christians need to be baptized. If you come to us and say you are already baptized, the priest will almost always take you at your word.

Old Catholic baptism includes both water and anointing with oil. If you want to become an Old Catholic and were baptized in one of the Protestant denominations that don't anoint, we will try to get you to accept a conditional baptism. It respects your original baptism but says "if you are not already baptized, then I baptize you…" and so forth.

Baptism is the only sacrament that can be performed by a person who is not ordained. The minister technically does not even have to be Christian! This is for emergencies,[57] of course. If someone is in danger of dying and asks to be baptized, you should comply without hesitation.

Old Catholics baptize infants, children and adults.

---

57 The technical term is "in extremis" (Latin).

FORM

At a minimum Baptism includes baptismal water (not "Holy Water" which is laced with salt) coming in contact with the person's scalp three times as the minister repeats the words of institution: "I baptize you in the name of the Father, the Son and the Holy Spirit."

Technically, the water should be allowed to drip all the way from scalp to the ground, but this is almost never practiced (especially if you are the one who has to clean up the floor or have a nun with a mop lurking in the shadows frowning menacingly at your drips).

There are drawings as old as the year 300 that show pouring of the water, rather than fully immersing the person in the water. Either works. If a convert to the Old Catholic Church wants to be dunked completely and there is a river nearby, that is perfectly acceptable.

In addition to the water, an Old Catholic Priest will anoint the person with Oil of the Catechumens, which is made from olive oil and consecrated by a bishop on the Thursday before Easter.[58]

MATTER

The priest blesses water used for baptism just before the liturgy. It is baptismal water, not "holy water" (which is heavily salted).

The words of institution that are required at all baptisms come from the end of the Gospel of Matthew. They are the final instructions from Jesus to his followers:

Then the eleven disciples went away into Galilee, to the mountain, which Jesus had appointed for them. When they saw Him, they worshiped Him; but some doubted. And Jesus came and spoke to them, saying, "All authority has been given to Me in

---

58 called Maundy Thursday in most church calendars

heaven and on earth.

> *"Go therefore and make disciples of all the nations,*
> *baptizing them in the name of the Father and of the*
> *Son and of the Holy Spirit, teaching them to observe*
> *all things that I have commanded you; and lo, I am*
> *with you always, even to the end of the age."*
>
> Matthew 28:16-20 (NKJV)

The anointing oil is Oil of the Catechumens.

INTENT

You can assume that the minister at a baptism intends for the action to be a valid baptism.

CONFIRMATION (CHRISMATION)

> *Now when the apostles who were at Jerusalem heard*
> *that Samaria had received the word of God, they sent*
> *Peter and John to them, who, when they had come*
> *down, prayed for them that they might receive the*
> *Holy Spirit. For as yet He had fallen upon none of*
> *them. They had only been baptized in the name of the*
> *Lord Jesus. Then they laid hands on them, and they*
> *received the Holy Spirit.*
>
> The Acts of the Apostles 8:14-17 (NKJV)

Confirmation is the passage of a child into adulthood. The liturgy is performed by a bishop, although the bishop customarily empowers priests to perform Confirmation if the person is in imminent danger of death.[59]

The Eastern Church calls this Sacrament Chrismation, and

---

59 "in extremis"

it is commonly administered to an infant immediately after baptism.

Catholics, including Old Catholics and Roman Catholics, wait until a child has reached the "age of reason" and has been instructed in the ways of the church. Jews have a rite similar in timing: bar mitzvah (boys) and bat mitzvah (girls). Some Reformed Jews actually call the service Confirmation, rather than its traditional name.

The Old Catholic Church teaches that when the bishop anoints the child, the Holy Spirit is called and descends into that child's soul as a permanent mark.

Although it is not a "must have" part of Confirmation, it is common for a child or convert to take on a Confirmation name. It is usually the name of a saint that hold special meaning for the person or who represents some admirable quality the person wants to work toward.

FORM

In the Old Catholic Church, a person must be able to understand the nature of Confirmation before it is allowed to occur. At a minimum, a child must be 7 years old. The child is commonly 14 to 16.

The bishop (or priest under very restricted circumstances) anoints the child or adult with Sacred Chrism.[60]

MATTER

The minister (almost always a bishop) draws a cross on a person's forehead using Sacred Chrism while saying: I sign thee

---

[60] A mixture of olive oil and balsam (which is a pasty by-product of the manufacture of essential oils). Sacred Chrism, like all of the church's anointing oils, are consecrated by the bishop on the Thursday before Easter. I know of one Old Catholic bishop who used to "spike" Chrism with a few drops of spikenard essential oil, one of the holy oils mentioned in the Christian Bible. It wasn't "kosher," but it certainly supercharged the oil.

with the sign of the cross + and I confirm thee with the chrism of salvation, in the Name of the Father + and of the Son, and of the Holy Ghost.

The bishop then strikes the person gently on the cheek, saying, Peace to you.

Intent

You can assume that the bishop at a Confirmation intends for the action to be a valid Confirmation.

Holy Orders

I have two critical things to say about ordination, before we jump into the nitty-gritty.

First, the North American Old Catholic Church has an excellent seminary, and it is accustomed to distance learning. If you are in Alaska for example, studying at our seminary will not be a problem. You will have to come for some in-person training: one weekend a year (otherwise you won't know how to say Mass as some things cannot be taught by distance learning). The point here is that we are not a "diploma mill," and we don't sell ordinations.

The second thing you need to know that absolutely everyone who becomes member of our clergy is subject to a criminal background check. If you are entrusted with any finances of the church, you are also subject to a credit check and regular audits of your books.

Neither of those points are intended to scare potential applicants, but I thought it best to mention those requirements before we get into the topic of ordinations and Holy Orders.

The Ordination of ministers goes all the way back to when Jesus told Cephas (the Aramaic name of the apostle we call Simon Peter) to drop what he was doing and follow. Jesus told Peter he would become a fisher of men.

Holy Orders is where the Tradition of the church is in the front of the Sacrament. The original apostles laid hands on others and sent them out to spread the Good News of Jesus.

Saul, who had once been a killer of Christians, was converted and took the name of Paul. The apostles ordained Paul. He took the word of Jesus beyond Israel and into the non-Jewish parts of the Roman Empire. Paul then passed his ordination on to others so that the ministry could continue even if he was in prison.

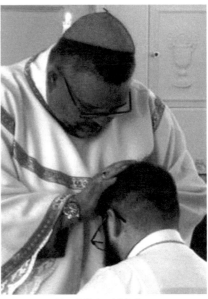

Abp. Michael V. Seneco
First presiding bishop of the North American Old Catholic Church

Every Catholic priest is ordained in an unbroken line that extends all the way back to the original apostles. This tradition is what makes us an Apostolic church. Not everyone who preaches outside our church carries the soul's mark of an apostle. The Old Catholic Church is very careful to assure that each of its deacons, priests and bishops are ordained with a carefully documented lineage of Apostolic Succession.

Protecting this unbroken line may not be a big deal to you, but it is a critical part of every bishop's job.

You probably already know that there are several levels or ranks of ordination: bishop, priest and deacon. There are actually more. They are divided into major and minor orders, with one level that is neither major nor minor. Each person who is in the seminary progresses through these Holy Orders. No Order is ever skipped, but a bishop may choose to ordain a person to multiple levels during a single ceremony.

Minor Orders

The Minor Orders are cleric, doorkeeper, reader, exorcist and acolyte. These are ecclesiastical in nature, which means they were invented by the church and are not actually Sacraments. Each imparts a stronger mark than the previous order, allowing the future minister to grow in grace as his or her studies continue.

The Old Catholic Church is a diverse group. We ordain men and women, lesbian and gays, married and celibate individuals. God doesn't discriminate, and neither do we. People are born female, and that is not some kind of mistake that makes Holy Orders impossible. People are born lesbian and gay, and that is not some kind of mistake that we should shun or avoid.

All except a few individuals are part-time ministers. Each has a day job because our priesthood pays little or nothing.

Not Minor, Not Major

There is a transitional order: subdeacon. It is not part of the group of minor orders, but it isn't a sacramental major order. The job of a subdeacon is to read the epistle during Mass. Subdeacons can wear a clerical shirt and use the term "Reverend" in front of his or her name. While the minor orders are for personal growth, being a subdeacon is the start of an individual's public ministry.

In a formal Mass, the subdeacon may wear a tunicle, a plain garment that is only worn by a subdeacon

The Major Orders are deacon, priest and bishop. Each rank involves a ritual ordination that is a Sacrament.

DEACON

The job of a deacon is to read and teach the gospel. When you see a priest reading the gospel or delivering a sermon, you just think the priest is reading and preaching. The priest is doing that only because he or she passed through the Order of Deacons. A deacon may be transitional (passing through to the priesthood) or permanent (not called to the priesthood).

Deacons wear what looks like a priest's stole, but the two ends are attached to each other. The deacon's stole hangs from one shoulder. In a formal Mass, a deacon may wear a dalmatic, which has the same silhouette as a subdeacon's tunicle but has more adornment. When a bishop performs an ordination, you can often catch a glance at the bishop wearing a dalmatic under his or her other liturgical dress. Once a deacon, always a deacon!

PRIEST

A priest's duty is to say Mass, to hear confession and offer Absolution, to witness marriages, to anoint the sick and to impart God's blessings. A priest always works at the direction of a bishop.

BISHOP

A bishop is the highest form of major orders (or its lowest order, depending on your point of view and level of humility). The job of each bishop includes saying Mass for everyone in his or her jurisdiction, to protect the Sacred Traditions of the church, to perform Confirmations and Holy Orders, and to administer the church.

Being a bishop is more complicated than it looks, especially in an old fashioned, traditional church such as the Old Catholic Church.

There are some other titles that are marks of authority but are not part of holy orders.

- An archdeacon in the Old Catholic Church is something like a monsignor in the Roman sect. Archdeacons are priests with extra duties.
- An archbishop is a bishop with additional responsibilities. Archbishops usually have a number of bishops in their care.

FORM

For the sacramental orders (deacon, priest and bishop), the form of the ordination must include a validly consecrated bishop with the authority to ordain, laying his or her hands on the head of the ordinand while saying **Receive the Holy Spirit for the office and duties of deacon** (or priest or bishop).

The bishop anoints the hands of a new priest.

The Sacrament of Holy Orders must always be performed at the public celebration of Mass. No "secret" ordination is ever valid, and it is up to the bishop to make sure this kind of thing never happens.

MATTER

The hands of the ordaining bishop must come into direct contact with the head of the ordinand while the bishop repeats the words of institution ("Receive the....")

INTENT

The bishop must intend to impart the Sacrament of Holy Orders (deacon, priest and bishop).

MATRIMONY

The Sacrament of Matrimony is the joining of two people for the sharing of a lifetime together and often for procreation.

The ministers of the Sacrament are the individuals being married. The priest (or bishop, or deacon in some cases) is there as the church's official witness.

The Old Catholic Church allows marriage between people who have been divorced and between people of the same gender. Matrimony is more correctly called the Solemnization of Matrimony. In the United States, it often includes civil marriage. An Old Catholic marriage, however, is *sometimes* not recognized by the civil authority: such as the union of two people of the same gender in a state that does not recognize LGBT marriage. The church recognizes it. In the eyes of the church, any marriage witnessed by a member of the clergy is a valid marriage regardless of that the government might state.

No Old Catholic priest is required to perform any individual marriage. Maybe the priest knows of a reason why the couple should not be married, or may the priest has issues with a mixed marriage (one member who is non-Christian) or with a same-gender marriage. That priest has an obligation to find another Old Catholic priest who will serve as the church's official witness.

In many cases, a priest will ask an engaged couple to come to one or more pre-marriage counseling sessions. This is up to the priest and the priest's bishop.

FORM

The Roman sect considers marriage to be a sacrament only when it is the union of a Catholic man and a Catholic woman. Rome goes so far as to say that no Roman Catholic youngster is allowed to date someone who is outside that faith. Modern adherents of the Roman rite don't usually follow the bishop's more harsh rules, of course.

The Old Catholic Church is not so rigid, but it is true that religion flows more freely when both parties share a similar Reality Map.

A marriage may take place during the celebration of a Nuptial Mass, but it may also occur as a simple ceremony outside of Mass. It is not necessary for marriage to take place inside a church building. There is no requirement for any other witnesses: the couple and the priest constitute a quorum. The civil authority may require additional witnesses.

MATTER

A marriage takes place when the two individuals express their intention freely and publicly and a priest, acting as the church's official witness, blesses the union.

INTENT

Both individuals must approach their union with full consent. No "shotgun wedding" is ever a valid sacrament.[61]

The Rites of Healing

ABSOLUTION

Confession is good for the soul, and confession along with its corresponding absolution is one of the Sacraments of the church.

There is a seal that protects what a person tells a priest during a Confession. There is no legal authority that can force a priest to repeat what is said during a confession. In fact, Church Law is quite blunt about a priest's treatment of information heard

---

61 Matrimonium facit consensus.

during a Confession:

> *V.06. (g) The sacramental seal is inviolable; therefore it is absolutely forbidden* (nefas est) *for a confessor to betray in any way a penitent in words or in any manner and for any reason.*
>
> Canons of the North American Old Catholic Church

For a good cause, a priest is allowed to withhold absolution. For example, if you tell a priest that you have killed someone, the priest may tell you to go turn yourself in and refuse absolution until you do that. The priest, however, would never be allowed to tell the police or anyone else what you did or even plan to do.

No forbidding is forbidden more than this. There's no talking to anyone for any reason. No exceptions. Period. End of story.

The Italian church requires its members to go to Confession at least once a year. The Old Catholic Church has no such rule, but will be quick to state that regular Confession and Absolution will make your spiritual growth smoother.

Absolution is the release from the bonds of sin. It marks your return to God's grace. Absolution is the actual Sacrament. Confession is what usually comes before Absolution.

FORM

There are three sets of words that the priest may employ for an Absolution. Each dates to the earliest days of the church.

1. *May the Almighty God have mercy on you, and forgive your sins, bring you to life everlasting. Amen.* Then, lifting his right hand towards the penitent, the priest continues: *May the Almighty and Merciful God grant you pardon, absolution, and remission of your sins.*

2. *I absolve you from your sins in the name of the Father, and of the Son, and of the Holy Ghost. Amen.* While repeating the names of the Trinity, the

    priest makes the sign of the cross over the penitent.

3.   *May the Passion of Our Lord Jesus Christ, the merits of the Blessed Virgin Mary and of all the Saints, what good you have done or what evil you have suffered be to you for the remission of your sins, growth in grace and the reward of everlasting life. Amen.*

The words can be in any language, but hopefully it is one understood by all. Latin would be the "go to" language if you cannot communicate using a common language.

The Italian church has an additional form used to bring back someone who had been excommunicated (suspended) from the church. The Old Catholic Church does not excommunicate people, so it does not use this fourth form.

Matter

Technically, Confession and Absolution are not tied so closely together that they cannot be separated. You already know that a priest is allowed to withhold Absolution. You can have Confession without Absolution: you might stop a priest on the street and say, "Hi, father. I just stole Johnny's Rolls Royce" and walk off. This is not going to go down as a Sacrament because you don't seems sorry you did it and because you did not ask for Absolution.

It is also possible for a priest to Absolve people who have not gone to Confession. This might happen when a group of soldiers are about to go into battle. It happens in old forms of Mass such as the form used in the Old Catholic Church just before the Communion rite.

Intent

There are two individuals involved in the Sacrament of Absolution. The priest must have the intent of imparting the Sacrament, and the recipient must be sorry for whatever sins he or she has committed.

UNCTION

Unction is the anointing of the sick. Just because it is the last Sacrament in this book doesn't mean it is the least important. Far from it: Unction is important — crucial, even — for our spiritual growth.

This is the Sacrament that is sometimes called "Last Rites" or "Extreme Unction," with the idea that it is given only to those who are about to die.

Nope.

Unction is for those who are sick in an everyday sort of way. It can be for a physical, emotional or spiritual sickness. What's more, it is possible to receive the Sacrament of Unction for the benefit of someone else. That other person doesn't have to request it or even know about it. It is better to give than to receive, you know.

FORM

A priest is the minister at the Sacrament of Unction. He or she anoints the forehead of the person and praying for the Holy Spirit to flow down into the person.

Unction (Rogier van der Weyden, 1399-1464)

When Unction is performed in extremis (at the danger of death), the priest anoints all five external senses (eyes, ears, nostrils, lips and hands) using word similar to "What sins you have committed by sight, they are forgiven" and so forth. When it is impossible to come into direct contact with the person's skin (bandages, communicable disease, etc), it is valid for the priest to draw a cross over the sick person's sense organs using his thumb and Oil of the Infirm.[62]

The Unction in extremis concludes with a large cross drawn over the entire person with the priest saying "What sins you have committed in spirit and soul, they are forgiven."

There are other prayers, of course, but these actions are the bare necessities.

MATTER

The oil used at Unction is Oil of the Infirm. Traditional anointing oils included olive oil, spikenard and others. The practice today is to use olive oil that is consecrated by a bishop specifically for use during the Sacrament of Unction.

Presence of the oil is required, but touching of the sick person's skin is preferred but not absolutely required.

Anointing is mentioned explicitly in the book of James in the New Testament.

---

62 Oil of the Infirm (OI) is used. This is one of the three sacred oils of the church. It is pure olive oil, consecrated specifically for use at Unction by the bishop on the Thursday before Easter. Consecration is a kind of strong blessing that sets the oil apart for sacred use. After the oil is consecrated by the bishop, it can never be used for mundane things like salads. In other words, you can't "un-consecrate" an oil.

Prayer

We are told to pray without ceasing. Part of me is conflicted in telling you this, because so many of us confuse God for Santa Claus. Yet our instructions are clear: pray without ceasing.

That said, the idea of praying for a winning lottery ticket gives me the creeps. If you feel called to do so, then you should go for it. I don't like the idea.

On the other hand, Jesus told a parable about a squeaky wheel that seems to put me on the wrong side of the lottery-prayer debate.

> Then He spoke a parable to them, that men always ought to pray and not lose heart, saying: "There was in a certain city a judge who did not fear God nor regard man. Now there was a widow in that city; and she came to him, saying, 'Get justice for me from my adversary.' And he would not for a while; but afterward he said within himself, 'Though I do not fear God nor regard man, yet because this widow troubles me I will avenge her, lest by her continual coming she weary me.'"
>
> Then the Lord said, "Hear what the unjust judge said. And shall God not avenge His own elect who cry out

day and night to Him, though He bears long with
them? I tell you that He will avenge them speedily.
Nevertheless, when the Son of Man comes, will He
really find faith on the earth?"

Luke 18:1-8 (NKJV)

The widow was "praying" for justice, and even though the judge wasn't a fair judge, she finally wore him down. I always assumed that the passage was about my mother. She was very persistent when she wanted something… over and over and over: the same thing. "Clean your room."

We are taught by scripture to pray to God, especially using the name of the Son. A common ending to a prayer directed to God the Father is:

We ask this through Christ, thy Son and our Lord,
who lives and reigns with You and the Holy Spirit,
world without end. Amen.

We might also pray to the Holy Spirit, for one of the graces of the Spirit.

The Pater Noster

We were taught by Jesus on the way to pray:

ENGLISH

Our Father, which art in heaven, hallowed be thy
name; thy kingdom come; thy will be done, in earth
as it is in heaven. Give us this day our daily bread.
And forgive us our trespasses, as we forgive them that
trespass against us. And lead us not into temptation;
but deliver us from evil.

> *Pater noster, qui es in caelis: sanctificetur Nomen*
> *Tuum; adveniat Regnum Tuum; fiat voluntas Tua,*
> *sicut in caelo, et in terra. Panem nostrum cotidianum*
> *da nobis hodie; et dimitte nobis debita nostra, Sicut et*
> *nos dimittimus debitoribus nostris; et ne nos inducas*
> *in tentationem; sed libera nos a Malo.*

Jesus spoke Aramaic, which is sort of a street Hebrew. The gospels were originally written in Greek. Latin came later.

The Lord's Prayer doesn't survive in the dialect of Aramaic that Jesus would have spoken. The closest we have is Syriac Aramaic, which is close enough to the original that Jesus and His followers would probably understand it.

Some Protestants add a pious doxology at the end of the prayer, and it is okay for them to do so. The words were common with Jews at the time of Jesus, but they were not part of the prayer Jesus taught his disciples to pray:

> *For thine is the kingdom and the power and the glory*
> *for ever and ever.*

I don't really like to pull verses out of the Bible to make a point, especially when they were written by Saint Paul, but Paul makes a couple of good points on prayer:

> *Therefore I exhort first of all that supplications,*
> *prayers, intercessions, and giving of thanks be made*
> *for all men, for kings and all who are in authority,*
> *that we may lead a quiet and peaceable life in all god-*
> *liness and reverence. For this is good and acceptable*
> *in the sight of God our Savior, who desires all men to*
> *be saved and to come to the knowledge of the truth.*
> *For there is one God and one Mediator between God*
> *and men, the Man Christ Jesus, who gave Himself a*

*ransom for all, to be testified in due time, for which
I was appointed a preacher and an apostle — I am
speaking the truth in Christ and not lying — a teacher
of the Gentiles in faith and truth.*

I Timothy 2:1-7 (NKJV)

*Rejoice always, pray without ceasing, in everything
give thanks; for this is the will of God in Christ Jesus
for you.*

I Thessalonians 5:16-18 (NKJV)

The Jesus Prayer

When you pray, your whole being is focused on God. There is a really simple prayer, called the Jesus Prayer. Some religious people try to have the Jesus Prayer going on inside their head all the time.

There are several forms of the Jesus Prayer:

Lord Jesus

Lord Jesus, have mercy on me.

Christ Jesus, have mercy on me, a sinner.

The Jesus Prayer is very important in the Eastern churches of Christianity. They sometimes call it the Prayer of the Mind.

The sentiment comes from the Gospel of Luke:

*He spake this parable unto certain which trusted in
themselves that they were righteous, and despised
others:*

*Two men went up into the temple to pray; the one
a Pharisee, and the other a publican. The Pharisee
stood and prayed thus with himself, God, I thank thee,
that I am not as other men are, extortioners, unjust,*

adulterers, or even as this publican. I fast twice in the week, I give tithes of all that I possess.

And the publican, standing afar off, would not lift up so much as his eyes unto heaven, but smote upon his breast, saying, God be merciful to me a sinner.

I tell you, this man went down to his house justified rather than the other: for every one that exalteth himself shall be abased; and he that humbleth himself shall be exalted.

Luke 18:9-14 (KJV)

The prayer itself most likely originated by the Desert Fathers, monks who lived in the deserts of Egypt between the years 300 and 500. It is a kind of antidote to Adam's pride because keeping the prayer in mind keeps your mind bound to God.

At a minimum, you can consider the Jesus prayer to be the Christian mantra (a sound repeated because it can bring spiritual change). Unlike a traditional non-Christian mantra — such as OM — which depends on a particular sound, the Jesus prayer can be said in whatever language is handy.

The Jesus Prayer can and will grow on you with practice. Romanian monks list nine levels that the prayer can take you through: prayer of the lips, prayer of the mouth, prayer of the tongue, prayer of the voice, prayer of the mind, prayer of the heart, active prayer, all-seeing prayer and contemplative prayer.

It must be similar to what Mother Theresa of Calcutta said when she was asked what she prayed for. She said she didn't pray for anything. She just listened. When asked what God said, she said God didn't say anything either. God just listened. There is no prayer more deep that this union with God.

Saints

Some say that Catholics are wrong when they worship saints.

I absolutely agree! It is not correct to worship any saint or angel, not even the Theotokos (Blessed Virgin Mary). If there is worship to be done, we should worship God the Father, God the Son, and God the Holy Spirit.

Saints are those who have walked-the-walk in the past and whose life is worth of praise and remembrance. Saints are those holy people whose life we would do well to notice and follow.

The Blessed Virgin Mary would be a saint. Many in the Roman rite would consider her a kind of über-saint. If that is the way you feel, it is great. You are not required to venerate any particular individual.

In the past, every village would have its own collection of saints. Ireland had Patrick. Holland and Luxembourg have Willibrord. In Italy, you basically trip over saints in every village.

The people in Ireland would look at you goofy if you mentioned Saint Willibrord, while those in Holland would raise one eyebrow if you mentioned Saint Patrick.

Somewhere along the way, Rome got the idea that it should be the sole arbitrator of who was called a saint. What they were doing makes sense. They were trying to prevent abuse. Some saints, like Saint Christopher, were popular but probably never existed. Maybe they were an amalgam, a composite of two or more individuals that somebody thought would be a good match.

St. Willibrord (658-739)

Unfortunately, when you put a bureaucrat in charge of anything, the rules become so tedious that people lose sight of what is important. Today, only the bishop of Rome can declare somebody a saint. Before that happens, they make the poor dead guy go through an investigation by staff of clerics in the Vatican. The individual must be associated with a certain number of miracles. The Vatican even has someone who acts as the "Devil's Advocate" finding all the reasons why the person should never be listed as a saint. If the individual makes it past this team of white-lipped officials, the pope will say they are "Blessed" or "Venerable," which is a step below being called a saint. If nobody starts screaming foul and if miracles continue to be reported, the poor dead soul is finally listed as an official saint.

Nobody is required to accept what Rome says about who is or isn't a saint. Even Rome admits that such a thing is really under God's job description. What the word "saint" does is get you on a liturgical calendar, maybe worldwide or just in one country.

It is all very rigid, with rules and paperwork and committees and hearings and testimony.

Such a bother.

Look, if a group of Old Catholics come to me with word they want to start a church named after a local dead guy that everybody thinks lived a holy life and whose actions deserve to be followed, I am going to do everything in my power to approve that.

One of the Old Catholic parishes in Dallas, Texas, is named after St. Mychal Judge. He was the Franciscan fire department chaplain killed when Al Qaeda attacked the World Trade Center in New York City on September 11, 2001. He was active with fire fighters, with Dignity (a group of gay Roman Catholics), with those suffering from HIV/AIDS and those trying to kick one addiction or another. When he went out on a walk in the cold, he would often come back without the coat he had on when he left the Church of St. Francis, near Penn Station in Manhattan. When TWI flight 800 exploded over Long Island Sound, Father Judge was the one who was there for the families. Because he worked with LGBT Roman Catholics, there is no chance that Rome and its "Devil's Advocate" will ever let Mychal Judge be listed as an official saint of the Roman sect (and they have every right to act that way). On the other hand, the members of the Dallas church think Mychal Judge's life is worthy of copying. We should all work as tirelessly as Mychal Judge with people shunned by others and with people who serve as valiantly as fire fighters. I was thrilled to let the church be called Saint Mychal Judge Old Catholic Church.

So, we absolutely do not worship any saint. We can and do pray that a saint will intercede for us.

The church is the Mystical Body of Christ, and we believe there is a lot going on that is beyond the physical world we can touch. There is a spiritual component to the universe that we don't understand.

Is it really possible for us to get a personal message into the "hands" of a dead person who may or may not be part of the heavenly host?

I have no idea if that is possible, but I do know that the universe behaves as though it is possible. If it is an angel or spiritual being working some astral switchboard, so be it. How heaven works is something that is beyond my capacity to understand.

In fact, I don't even care how it works, but I do know that it does work.

I have faith that there is something going on. I have seen the results of whatever it is, and that is quite good enough for me.

Angels

The word angel comes to us from a Hebrew word that means messenger. Angels are in the New Testament when God has some kind of message that has to be delivered.

One of the first things the angel messenger "says" to the human is "Do not be afraid."

I'm sorry. If an angel with wings and a halo pops into my living room in the middle of Monday Night Football, I am going to be afraid. There is nothing that this poor messenger can say to stop my reaction.

Angels probably don't have wings. Bells don't ring when angels are awarded their wings (because they don't have wings).

The devil (also known as Lucifer) is an angel, according to Christian mythology. The word "Lucifer" means the "light-bearer." So the head "fallen" angel is actually the bearer of light.

Various rankings of angels are mentioned in the Bible and other spiritual writings: angels, archangels, thrones, dominations, powers, seraphim and cherubim. Some are thought to have specific traits Michael is a fighting archangel, for example.

The Angel of the Mass

One part of the celebration of the Eucharist is especially noteworthy. The text is awesome, and the thought is one of the most profound notions anywhere in religion.

Shortly after the Consecration of the Body and Blood of our Lord, the priest offers the following prayer:

We humbly beseech thee, almighty God: command these offerings to be brought by the hands of thy holy Angel to thine altar on high, in sight of thy divine majesty: that all we who at this partaking of the altar shall receive the most sacred Body and Blood of thy Son, may be fulfilled with all heavenly benediction and grace. Through the same Christ our Lord. Amen.

Súpplices te rogámus, omnípotens Deus: jube hæc perférri per manus sancti Angeli tui in sublíme altáre tuum, in conspéctu divínæ majestátis tuæ ut quotquot ex hac altáris participatióne sacrosánctum Fíii tui, Corpus et Sánguinem sumpsérimus, omni benedictióne cælésti et grátia repleámur. Per eúndem Christum Dóminum nostrum. Amen.

If the Eucharist is the most blessed and solemn gift ever given to mankind by God, what better sentiment can there be than to offer it back to God?

The liturgy used by the Liberal Catholic Church, which broke away from the Old Catholic Church in the early 20th Century is even more direct in its liturgy:

> *Wherefore, O Lord and heavenly Father, we Thy humble servants, bearing in mind the ineffable sacrifice of Thy Son, the mystery of His wondrous incarnation, His blessed passion, His mighty resurrection, and His triumphant ascension, do here make before Thy Divine Majesty the memorial which our Lord hath willed us to make, and we do offer unto Thee this, the*

most precious gift which Thou hast bestowed upon us: this pure Host, this holy Host, this glorious Host, the holy Bread of life ever-lasting, and the Chalice of eternal salvation.

This do we present before Thee in token of our love and of the perfect devotion and sacrifice of our minds and hearts to Thee; and we pray that Thou wouldst command Thy holy Angel to bear our oblation to Thine altar on high, there to be offered by Him who, as the eternal High Priest, forever offers Himself as the eternal Sacrifice.

You can find the entire Liberal Catholic liturgy as well as several others at the Old Catholic Library: www.global.org — freely available to you.

The Guardian Angel

The idea of a personal or private angel isn't new. There are references back into the 400s[63] that discuss angels assigned to individuals as their teacher or guide.

New Age teachers speak of Ascended Masters. Rosicrucian and Reiki practitioners deal with guides or go-betweens or advisors.

I once fired my guardian angel. No, I really did. Seriously. I

---

63 The earliest reference that I know is in the *Corpus Areopagiticum* of Pseudo-Dionysius the Areopagite.

got into a jam and felt this alleged angel must have been asleep or otherwise negligent. You can't sue a Guardian Angel, so I lit a candle and asked for a new angel to be assigned to my life.

Oh, yes I did, too. It was when I was in the 4th grade, and it tells you more about me than about the choirs of angels or their duties.

So, do we have guardian angels? Are there Ascended Masters whose job it is to guide human beings?

I have no idea, but the universe behaves as though they exist.

If we have some kind of alien being that corresponds with us using telepathy, is something beyond my interest. I am less interested in the actual nomenclature and source of spiritual beings than I am in knowing there is something to bail me out when (not if) I get myself into a mystical pickle (which happens with frightening regularity).

I secretly think my new/improved Guardian Angel is terrified of what mischief I will get into. Things around me just happen. It is like my angel takes care of things to keep my over-active and eager hands out of my spiritual machinery because they are the ones who will have to clean up the mess.

Whatever: it works nicely.

In the Jewish Scripture, an angel is assigned to look after Israel.[64] God told Moses that an angel would go before him.[65]

In the Christian Scripture, Jesus himself talks about angels guiding and guarding people.[66] Saint Paul calls them "ministering spirits."[67]

Guardian angels are all over the place in Christian and Jewish scripture and literature. Saints write about them. Jesus talked about them. I fire them when I don't like what they are doing. And so forth. And so on.

---

64 Exodus 12

65 Exodus 32

66 Matthew 18

67 Hebrews 1

When you find yourself stuck spiritually, try closing your eyes and saying a one word prayer that should snap your guardian angel into attention:

HELP!

Responding to that short prayer is the very job description of our ministering spirits, regardless of what their actual essence really is.

The Guardian Angel
Wilhelm von Kaulbach (1805-1874)

There is no better test of this than trying it. At no time am I asking you to take anything in this book as literal just because ink has touched paper.

I am suggesting that you use the wealth of spiritual tools at your disposal. I am saying that based on my own personal experience; there is nothing stronger or faster that assistance brought by God's messenger service: the angels.

The Sanctification of Time

The church year is divided into two halves.

The first part begins at Advent (the weeks before Christmas) and goes all the way through Easter and the Ascension (when Jesus Christ left earth). This half of the year covers the entire story of Jesus: birth, crucifixion, resurrection and ascension into heaven. The church concentrates on the *historical events*.

The other half of the year is all about us. We concentrate on taking the principles of Christianity and welding them to our daily life.

Part of the church calendar consists of fixed days. Christmas Day is always December 25th. Those are easy enough, but the biggest day of the Christmas year — Easter — almost takes a rocket scientist to calculate. In fact, I know someone who works at NASA (the US agencies that employees rocket scientists), and my friend just shrugged his shoulders when I asked him about Easter. Here is the way to calculate Easter: it is the first Sunday, following the first full moon, following the vernal (Spring) equinox.

Lent is the season before Easter. It is 40 days, beginning with Ash Wednesday. But wait: Sundays are not considered part of Lent, so you have to figure 40 days plus an additional collection of Sundays. Pre-Lent is the countdown to Lent itself.

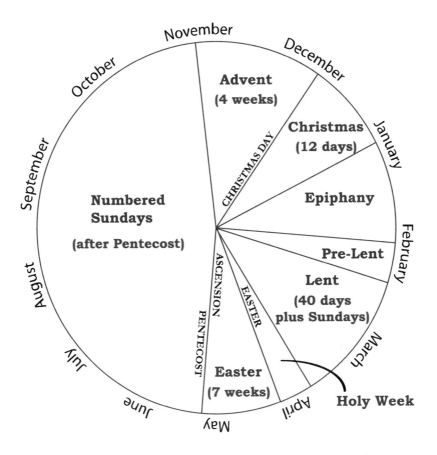

Where to Go from Here

At its root, the Old Catholic Church is here to protect believers from the excesses of other so-called "organized religions."

We trace our origins to the primitive Christian church in the lowlands, now called the Netherlands. Although it has always been independent, there was a rift between the Dutch Catholics and the Italian Catholics when the pope sent some Jesuits to find Peter Codde and drag him back to Rome for questioning and for trial.

Today's Old Catholic Church continues to act as a protector of innocent victims of larger religious bodies. We are not anti-Rome nor anti-pope. We admire the many great and holy people in that group.

We are certainly not anti-Lutheran. I just cannot sneer at a church group that produces someone like Johann Sebastian Bach.

We are neither anti-Baptist nor anti-Quaker either.

We are only against specific actions taken against believers.

If you have been hammered, neglected or rejected by one of the big Christian denominations, we invite you to join us.

Most of us are misfits. If you read the Bible, you will find that this is very precisely the sort of person that Jesus spent time with. Jesus was always getting in trouble for spending time with those who were not "fit" or "clean" or "proper."

If there is no Old Catholic Church where you live, we have a seminary that can train you to start such a church.

I hope to see you soon. Meanwhile, may you find the light you seek.

Appendix

The Apostles Creed

The Apostles Creed is one of the oldest statements of what Christians believe. It was mentioned by St. Ambrose in the year 390, and he considered it old even then.

The creed sums up what we believe in 12 statements about the faith. For all the in-fighting that goes on between Christian denominations, the Apostles Creed is one of the few things that almost every denomination accepts.

1. I believe in God, the Father almighty, creator of heaven and earth.

2. I believe in Jesus Christ, his only Son, our Lord.

3. He was conceived by the power of the Holy Spirit and born of the Virgin Mary.

4. He suffered under Pontius Pilate, was crucified, died, and was buried.

5. He descended into hell. On the third day he rose again.

6. He ascended into heaven and is seated at the right hand of the Father.

7.   He will come again to judge the living and the dead.

8.   I believe in the Holy Spirit,

9.   the holy catholic Church, the communion of saints,

10.   the forgiveness of sins,

11.   the resurrection of the body,

12.   and life everlasting. Amen.

Declaration of Ütrecht of 1889

Old Catholics have been an identifiable group since the late 700s in the Netherlands. They always looked to the Roman Pontiff as a leader, the Patriarch of the Western Church. Many Old Catholics still look at the pope as a patriarch. All Old Catholics reject the idea that the pope is anything else. There's no infallibility. There's no "my way or the highway."

When Roman bishops met in the Vatican for a council, they crossed the line. The meeting happened between 1869 and 1870. The pope got them to sign papers agreeing that the pope could speak without error (infallibility) on matters of church doctrine. Several bishops – including all the Old Catholic bishops – walked out of the proceedings.

Several bishops got together in the Netherlands in 1889. This council of bishops produced a document that is the foundation of today's Old Catholic Church.

> *We adhere faithfully to the Rule of Faith laid down by St. Vincent of Lerins in these terms:* Id teneamus, quod ubique, quod semper, quod ab omnibus creditum est; hoc est etenim vere proprieque catholicum.[68]

---

68 "We must hold fast to that faith which has been held everywhere, always, and by all the faithful."

For this reason we preserve in professing the faith of the primitive Church, as formulated in the oecumenical symbols and specified precisely by the unanimously accepted decisions of the Oecumenical Councils held in the undivided Church of the first thousand years.

We therefore reject the decrees of the so-called Council of the Vatican, which were promulgated July 18th, 1870, concerning the infallibility and the universal Episcopate of the Bishop of Rome, decrees which are in contradiction with the faith of the ancient Church, and which destroy its ancient canonical constitution by attributing to the Pope the plentitude of ecclesiastical powers over all Dioceses and over all the faithful. By denial of this primatial jurisdiction we do not wish to deny the historical primacy, which several Oecumenical[69] Councils and Fathers of the ancient Church have attributed to the Bishop of Rome by recognizing him as the primus inter pares.[70]

We also reject the dogma of the Immaculate Conception promulgated by Pius IX in 1854 in defiance of the Holy Scriptures and in contradiction to the tradition of the centuries.

As for other Encyclicals published by the Bishops of Rome in recent times for example, the Bulls Unigenitus and Auctorem fidei , and the Syllabus of 1864, we reject them on all such points as are in contradiction

---

69 Oecumenical is the oldtymie way of spelling Ecumenical. It basically means the universal and undivided church. The word is particularly brutal when you try to parse back through its etymology: late 16c., "representing the entire (Christian) world," formed in English as an ecclesiastical word, from L.L. oecumenicus "general, universal," from Gk. oikoumenikos, from he oikoumene ge "the inhabited world (as known to the ancient Greeks); the Greeks and their neighbors considered as developed human society," from oikoumenos, present passive participle of oikein "inhabit," from oikos "house, habitation" [etymonline.com]

70 first among equals (something like a Patriarch in the Eastern church)

with the doctrine of the primitive Church, and we do not recognize them as binding on the consciences of the faithful. We also renew the ancient protests of the Catholic Church of Holland against the errors of the Roman Curia, and against its attacks upon the rights of national Churches.

We refuse to accept the decrees of the Council of Trent in matters of discipline, and as for the dogmatic decisions of that Council we accept them only so far as they are in harmony with the teaching of the primitive Church.

Considering that the Holy Eucharist has always been the true central point of Catholic worship, we consider it our right to declare that we maintain with perfect fidelity the ancient Catholic doctrine concerning the Sacrament of the Altar, by believing that we receive the Body and Blood of our Saviour Jesus Christ under the species of bread and wine. The Eucharistic celebration in the Church is neither a continual repetition nor a renewal of the expiatory sacrifice which Jesus offered once for all upon the Cross: but it is a sacrifice because it is the perpetual commemoration of the sacrifice offered upon the Cross, and it is the act by which we represent upon earth and appropriate to ourselves the one offering which Jesus Christ makes in Heaven, according to the Epistle to the Hebrews 9:11-12, for the salvation of redeemed humanity, by appearing for us in the presence of God (Heb. 9:24). The character of the Holy Eucharist being thus understood, it is, at the same time, a sacrificial feast, by means of which the faithful in receiving the Body and Blood of our Saviour, enter into communion with one another (I Cor. 10:17).

We hope that Catholic theologians, in maintaining the faith of the undivided Church, will succeed in establishing an agreement upon questions which have been controverted ever since the divisions which arose between the Churches. We exhort the priests under our jurisdiction to teach, both by preaching and by the instruction of the young, especially the essential Christian truths professed by all the Christian confessions, to avoid, in discussing controverted doctrines, any violation of truth or charity, and in word and deed to set an example to the members.

By maintaining and professing faithfully the doctrine of Jesus Christ, by refusing to admit those errors which by the fault of men have crept into the Catholic Church, by laying aside the abuses in ecclesiastical matters, together with the worldly tendencies of the hierarchy, we believe that we shall be able to combat efficaciously the great evils of our day, which are unbelief and indifference in matters of religion.

Signed in Ütrecht, 24th September 1889
  +Johannes Heykamp, Bishop of Ütrecht
  +Casparus Johannes Rinkel
  +Cornelius Diependaal, Bishop of Deventer
  +Joseph Hubert Reinkens, Bishop of Germany
  +Eduard Herzog, Bishop of Switzerland

J. Heykamp   C. Rinkel   C. Diependaal J. H. Reinkens   E. Herzog

Fourteen Theses

Old Catholic bishops met in a council in Bonn, Germany, between September 14 and 16, 1874. They drafted a statement of the fundamental teachings of the Old Catholic Church.

1. *We agree that the apocryphal or deutero-canonical[71] books of the Old Testament are not of the same canonicity as the books contained in the Hebrew Canon.*

2. *We agree that no translation of Holy Scripture can claim an authority superior to that of the original text.*

3. *We agree that the reading of Holy Scripture in the vulgar[72] tongue cannot be lawfully forbidden.*

4. *We agree that, in general, it is more fitting, and in accordance with the spirit of the Church, that the Liturgy should be in the tongue understood by the people.*

5. *We agree that Faith working by Love, not Faith without Love, is the means and condition of Man's justification before God.*

6. *Salvation cannot be merited by "merit of condignity,"[73] because there is no proportion between the infinite worth of salvation promised*

---

71 Deuterocanonical literally means "between the canons." It includes Tobit, Judith, Wisdom of Solomon, Sirach (Ecclesiasticus), Baruch, and the Maccabees. It also includes some additional text in the books of Esther and Daniel. These books and additions are not part of the Jewish Bible.

72 The word just means the common language: French in France, strange-sounding English in England, etc.

73 Merit of condignity is a phrase that comes to us from St. Thomas Aquinas. It means you are awarded a place in heaven because of all the good works you did while alive. It also means that God is giving you more of a reward than you could have earned.

by God and the finite worth of man's works.

7. *We agree that the doctrine of* opera super-erogationis[74] *and of a thesaurus meritorum sanctorum, i.e., that the overflowing merits of the Saints can be transferred to others, either by the rulers of the Church, or by the authors of the good works themselves, is untenable.*

8. *We acknowledge that the number of the sacraments was fixed at seven, first in the <u>twelfth century</u>, and then was received into the general teaching of the Church, not as tradition coming down from the Apostles or from the earliest times, but as the result of theological speculation.*

 Catholic theologians acknowledge, and we acknowledge with them, that Baptism and the Eucharist are "principalia, praecipus, eximia salutis nostrae sacramenta."[75]

9. *The Holy Scriptures being recognized as the primary rule of Faith, we agree that the gen-*

---

74 "Opera supererogationis" means works that are above the minimum requirement. The idea is that you can get into heaven by following God's rules, but there are perks for going beyond the basic rule. And, behold, one came and said unto him, Good Master, what good thing shall I do, that I may have eternal life? And he said unto him, Why callest thou me good? there is none good but one, that is, God: but if thou wilt enter into life, keep the commandments. He saith unto him, Which? Jesus said, Thou shalt do no murder, Thou shalt not commit adultery, Thou shalt not steal, Thou shalt not bear false witness, honour thy father and thy mother: and, Thou shalt love thy neighbour as thyself. The young man saith unto him, All these things have I kept from my youth up: what lack I yet? Jesus said unto him, If thou wilt be perfect, go and sell that thou hast, and give to the poor, and thou shalt have treasure in heaven: and come and follow me. But when the young man heard that saying, he went away sorrowful: for he had great possessions. Then said Jesus unto his disciples, Verily I say unto you, That a rich man shall hardly enter into the kingdom of heaven. And again I say unto you, It is easier for a camel to go through the eye of a needle, than for a rich man to enter into the kingdom of God. [Matthew 19:16-24]

75 original, distinguished, and extraordinary sacraments that exist for our benefit

uine tradition, i.e. the unbroken transmission partly oral, partly in writing of the doctrine delivered by Christ and the Apostles is an authoritative source of teaching for all successive generations of Christians. This tradition is partly to be found in the consensus of the great ecclesiastical bodies standing in historical continuity with the primitive Church, partly to be gathered by scientific method from the written documents of all centuries.

We acknowledge that the Church of England, and the Churches derived from her, have maintained unbroken the Episcopal succession.

10. *We reject the new Roman doctrine of the Immaculate Conception of the Blessed Virgin Mary, as being contrary to the tradition of the first thirteen centuries according to which Christ alone is conceived without sin.*[76]

11. *We agree that the practice of confession of sins before the congregation or a Priest, together with the exercise of the power of the keys, has come down to us from the primitive Church, and that, purged from the abuses and free from constraint, it should be preserved in the Church.*

12. *We agree that "indulgences" can only refer to penalties actually imposed by the Church*

---

76 This is the dogma announced by Pope Pius IX in 1854. He said it is a teaching that all Roman adherents must accept because the dogma was pronounced by the pope, and no pope can make an error on dogma. Pius then convened a council of Roman bishops to confirm that popes can say something is dogma without any chance of error.

herself.[77]

13.   *We acknowledge that the practice of the commemoration of the faithful departed, i.e. the
calling down of a richer outpouring of Christ's
grace upon them, has come down to us from
the primitive Church, and is to be preserved in
the Church.*

14.   *The Eucharistic celebration in the Church is
not a continuous repetition or renewal of the
propitiatory sacrifice offered once for ever
by Christ upon the cross; but its sacrificial
character consists in this, that it is the permanent memorial of it, and a representation and
presentation on earth of that one oblation of
Christ for the salvation of redeemed mankind,
which according to the Epistle to the Hebrews
(9:11,12), is continuously presented in heaven
by Christ, who now appears in the presence of
God for us (9:24).*

*While this is the character of the Eucharist in refer-
ence to the sacrifice of Christ, it is also a sacred feast,
wherein the faithful, receiving the Body and Blood of
our Lord, have communion one with another (I Cor.
10:17).*

---

77 One example: a pope sold indulgences (get out of purgatory coupons) to pay for
St. Peters Basilica. Abuses of absolution were a big part in Martin Luther's com-
plaints against Rome, back in the 1500s.

For more information

The North American Old Catholic Church
http://www.naOldCatholic.com

The Old Catholic Library
http://www.global.org

Saint Wolbodo Seminary
http://www.wolbodo.org

Bibliography

Book of Common Prayer. Oxford: Oxford University Press, 1928.

"Canons of the North American Old Catholic Church." The Old Catholic Library. 2009. http://global.org/Pub/NAOCC_Canons.asp.

Chrysostom, John. *Divine Liturgy of St. John Chrysostom*. 5th Century. http://global.org/Pub/JC_Liturgy.asp (accessed November 2009).

Cochrane, Charles Norris. *Christianity and Classical Culture: A Study of Thought and Action from Augustus to Augustine*. New York: Oxford University Press, 1974.

Gillquist, Peter E., Alan Wallerstedt, Joseph Allen, Michel Najim, J. N. Sparks, and Theodore Stylianopoulos. *Oxford Study Byble: New Testament and Psalms, The*. Nashville, TN: Thomas Nelson Publishers, 1993.

Hexham, Irving. *Concise Dictionary of Religion*. Vancouver, BC: Regent College Publishing, 1993.

Lossky, Vladimir. *Orthodox Theology: An Introduction*. Crestwood, NY: St Vladimirs Seminary Press, 1989.

Meldenius, Rupertus. *Paraenesis votiva pro pace ecclesiae ad theologos Augustanae confessionis auctore Ruperto Meldenio Theologo.* Rottenburg, 1626.

Meyendorff, John. *Gregory Palamas: The Triads.* Mahwah, NJ: Paulist Press, 1983.

New King James Bible (NKJV). Nashville, TN: Thomas Nelson, Inc., 1982.

North American Orthodox-[Roman] *Catholic Theological Consultation.* "Baptism and "Sacramental Economy"." National Conference of [Roman] Catholic Bishops. 6 3, 1999. http://www.usccb.org/seia/agreed.shtml (accessed 9 1, 2009).

Rankin, Jim. *A Divine and Healing Path.* San Francisco, CA: North American Old Catholic Church, 2009.

About the Author

Archbishop Wynn Wagner is the Coadjutor Emeritus of the North American Old Catholic Church until his retirement in 2010. He also served as the Regionary Bishop of that denomination's Southern Province and is a past president of the Worldwide Conference of Old Catholic Churches.

He studied at Texas Christian University and St. Alban Theological Seminary. St. Wolbodo Seminary awarded him a ThD.

In 2012, the AIDS Global Education Information System (AEGiS: www.aegis.org) awarded him their Health, Human Rights and Humanitarian Award marking a lifetime of humanitarian work.

Since his retirement, Dr. Wagner has abandoned the crimson robes of an archbishop in favor of the tie-dyed t-shirts that speak to his inner hippie.

He has written and/or edited over 20 books.

Index

A CATECHISM
of the Liberal Catholic Church

Archbishop Wynn Wagner

FOURTH EDITION

The Divine & Healing Path:
An Old Catholic Catechism

Bishop Elijah (Jim Rankin)
with a foreword by Archbishop Wynn Wagner

ARCHBISHOP
CHARLES WEBSTER LEADBEATER

A Textbook of
Theosophy

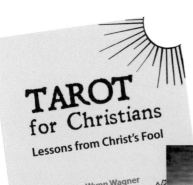

TAROT
for Christians
Lessons from Christ's Fool

Archbishop Wynn Wagner

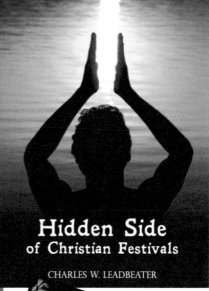

Hidden Side
of Christian Festivals

CHARLES W. LEADBEATER

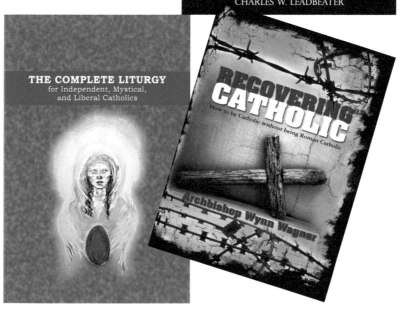

THE COMPLETE LITURGY
for Independent, Mystical,
and Liberal Catholics

RECOVERING
CATHOLIC
How to be Catholic without being Roman Catholic

Archbishop Wynn Wagner

Made in United States
Cleveland, OH
03 April 2025

15764586R00090